THE CAMBRIDGE BIBLE COMMENTARY

NEW ENGLISH BIBLE

GENERAL EDITORS

P. R. ACKROYD, A. R. C. LEANEY, J. W. PACKER

THE LETTERS OF JOHN
AND JAMES

D0927708

THE
LETTERS OF JOHN
AND JAMES

COMMENTARY ON
THE THREE LETTERS OF JOHN AND
THE LETTER OF JAMES

BY

R. R. WILLIAMS

Bishop of Leicester

CAMBRIDGE
AT THE UNIVERSITY PRESS
1965

PUBLISHED BY
THE SYNDICS OF THE CAMBRIDGE UNIVERSITY PRESS

Bentley House, 200 Euston Road, London, N.W. 1
American Branch: 32 East 57th Street, New York 22, N.Y.
West African Office: P.O. Box 33, Ibadan, Nigeria

CAMBRIDGE UNIVERSITY PRESS

1965

GENERAL EDITORS' PREFACE

The aim of this series is to provide the text of the New English Bible closely linked to a commentary in which the results of modern scholarship are made available to the general reader. Teachers and young people preparing for such examinations as the General Certificate of Education at Ordinary or Advanced Level in Britain, and similar qualifications elsewhere have been especially kept in mind. The commentators have been asked to assume no specialized theological knowledge, and no knowledge of Greek and Hebrew. Bare references to other literature and multiple references to other parts of the Bible have been avoided. Actual quotations have been given as often as possible.

Within these quite severe limits each commentator will attempt to set out the main findings of recent New Testament scholarship, and to describe the historical background to the text. The main theological content of the New Testament will also be critically discussed.

Much attention has been given to the form of the volumes. The aim is to produce books each of which will be read consecutively from first to last page. The introductory material leads naturally into the text, which itself leads into the alternating sections of commentary. By this means it is hoped that each book will be easily read and remain in the mind as a unity.

The series will be prefaced by a volume—*Understanding the New Testament*—which will outline the larger historical background, say something about the growth and transmission of the text, and answer the question 'Why should we study the New Testament?' Another volume—*The New Testament Illustrated*—will contain maps, diagrams and photographs.

P.R.A.
A.R.C.L.
J.W.P.

EDITOR'S PREFACE

I need only to express gratitude to my encouragers and helpers—to my wife, as always; to Professor Moule for keeping up my confidence; to the General Editors and the C.U.P. for their careful scrutinies; and to my former secretary, Miss Anne Bavin, for so cheerfully typing my manuscript.

R.R.L.

CONTENTS

THREE LETTERS OF JOHN

✻ ✻ ✻ ✻ ✻ ✻ ✻ ✻ ✻ ✻ ✻ ✻ ✻

How the Church has used the Letters *page* 3
What the Letters are about 6
1 John 7
The situation in view 9
2 John 11
3 John 12
The relation of the Johannine writings to each other, 13
and problems of their authorship

✻ ✻ ✻ ✻ ✻ ✻ ✻ ✻ ✻ ✻ ✻ ✻ ✻

Recall to Fundamentals (1 John) 16
Truth and Love (2 John) 62
Trouble in the Church (3 John) 67

✻ ✻ ✻ ✻ ✻ ✻ ✻ ✻ ✻ ✻ ✻ ✻ ✻

A LETTER OF JAMES

✻ ✻ ✻ ✻ ✻ ✻ ✻ ✻ ✻ ✻ ✻ ✻ ✻

The men called James in the New Testament 75
The Letter of James and other New Testament writings 84
The use of James in the early centuries of the Church 91
Conclusions 93

✻ ✻ ✻ ✻ ✻ ✻ ✻ ✻ ✻ ✻ ✻ ✻ ✻

Practical Religion (James) 96

✻ ✻ ✻ ✻ ✻ ✻ ✻ ✻ ✻ ✻ ✻ ✻ ✻

INDEX OF NAMES AND TOPICS 143

THREE LETTERS OF JOHN

THREE LETTERS OF
JOHN

✳ ✳ ✳ ✳ ✳ ✳ ✳ ✳ ✳ ✳ ✳ ✳ ✳

HOW THE CHURCH HAS USED THE LETTERS

Towards the end of the New Testament are three books, one of five chapters, two of one chapter, called respectively the first, second and third letters of John. For the last fifteen hundred years or so you would have found these three books included whenever a manuscript or book claimed to contain the complete New Testament. The famous Codex Sinaiticus (now in the British Museum), a manuscript dating from the fourth century, contains these three books. The Council of Carthage, held in A.D. 397 and at which Augustine was present, gave a list of canonical scriptures (i.e. scriptures accepted as authoritative by the Church) including 1, 2 and 3 John almost in their present position in the New Testament. They are also clearly listed in a 'Festal Letter' (an Easter greeting to fellow-bishops) of Athanasius, the great bishop of Alexandria, written in the year A.D. 367, in the course of which he gives a list of the canonical books as he and his church received them.

By the end of the fourth century, then, we can state that all three books were well established as part of the New Testament and were regarded as coming from the pen of 'John', who was commonly taken to be the writer of the Fourth Gospel and often also the writer of Revelation; and this writer was further taken to be that John, one of the twelve disciples of Jesus, thought to be referred to in the Fourth Gospel as the Beloved Disciple—'the disciple whom Jesus loved' (John 21:20).

Doubts, however, were widespread about the exact status of these letters, especially that of the two short ones. In the region of Syria, for instance, it was not till about A.D. 500 that the three books firmly found their place in the Canon. In the Syriac translation of the Bible, known as the Peshitta, there were only three *general* or *catholic* letters (i.e. letters addressed to undefined or very extensive communities, instead of named local churches or individuals), those of James, 1 Peter and 1 John. One cannot help wondering whether it seemed attractive to have just three letters, each bearing names strongly reminiscent of the three 'special' disciples, Peter, James, and John. Primitive thought would not distinguish as clearly as we do between James the disciple and apostle and James, 'the Lord's brother' (see the introductory material to the Letter of James, pp. 75–83 of this book).

In western circles Jerome, the great Latin scholar and teacher, in a work called *The Lives of Illustrious Men* (written in A.D. 392 at Bethlehem) states plainly that the Gospel of John was written by the apostle, the son of Zebedee, as was also the first letter. The other two letters (our 2 and 3 John) he describes thus: '[They] are said to be the work of John the presbyter, to the memory of whom another sepulchre is shown at Ephesus to the present day, though some think that there are two memorials of this same John the Evangelist'. That the first and the two latter letters did not receive the same total acceptance is reflected in a document known as the Mommsen Canon (after the man who discovered it). This gives the Canon as received in Africa about A.D. 360. The relevant part says (in Latin) 'Letters of John, 3, 350 verses' (i.e. 350 lines) under which someone has written, 'only one'. The difference of opinion around this period was probably based not only on different estimates of individual books as such, but on the appeal, on the one hand, of a three-book scheme for the general letters (1 Peter, 1 John and James) and, on the other, of a seven-book canon, these three, plus 2 Peter, 2 and 3 John, and Jude. The idea of having seven letters evidently also appealed to the author of Revelation, who begins his book with letters to seven different churches (Rev. 1: 4).

4

Now we can steadily work back as far as possible towards the time of the actual writing of the three books.

An important landmark appears in the famous *History of the Church*, written by Eusebius, bishop of Caesarea about A.D. 325. Eusebius includes the 'former' (i.e. first) letter of John among the 'accepted' writings, but puts 2 and 3 John among 'disputed' writings 'whether they belong to the Evangelist or to another person of the same name' (*History*, III. 25. 2, 3). Elsewhere (*History*, VI. 25) Eusebius quotes Origen, the great scholar of Alexandria and Caesarea who had died about seventy years earlier. Origen's statement is singularly obscure and ambiguous, but he *seems* to say that letters two and three are of doubtful authenticity. In referring both to the Gospel and Revelation he apparently omits clear reference to the first letter, but it is well known to him and frequently quoted in his writings.

Towards A.D. 200 we have the list contained in the so-called *Muratorian Fragment*—it tells us the Canon of the Roman church of that period. (It was called Muratorian after an Italian, Muratori, who discovered it in the eighteenth century.) This fragment quotes precisely from 1 John 1: 1, and later says 'the couple bearing the name of John are accepted in the Catholic [Church]'. Again it is not entirely clear whether the Canon includes letters 1, 2, and 3 or only 1 and *either 2 or 3*. There is some evidence that 1 and 2 John were translated into Latin from the original Greek at a different time from 3 John. If so, it suggests that 'the couple' referred to in the *Muratorian Fragment* may be 1 and 2 John.

Earlier, Irenaeus, who had come from the East, and later worked in southern Gaul, had referred to 1 John (using the words 'in his epistle') but he also *quoted*, apparently meaning to quote from 1 John, words which undoubtedly come from 2 John 7, 8 (*Against Heresies*, III. xvi. 5 and 8).

Clement of Alexandria (say A.D. 150 to A.D. 216) recognizes at least two letters and uses the first letter freely.

Papias, bishop of Hierapolis, about A.D. 140, according to

Irenaeus, used quotations from the first letter, and used a phrase ('The Truth itself') which happens to occur in 3 John 12.

Polycarp, bishop of Smyrna, writing about A.D. 108 certainly quotes 1 John 4: 2 almost word for word. His actual words are 'Everyone who does not confess that Jesus Christ has come in the flesh is Antichrist, and whoever does not confess the witness of the cross is of the devil'. The last words are reminiscent of 1 John 3: 8.

The earliest *possible* reference to 1 John is in Clement of Rome's letter to Corinth (A.D. 96)where Clement twice uses the phrase 'made perfect in love' (cf. 1 John 2: 5 and 4: 18).

We have now covered most of the references to these letters in the three centuries, A.D. 100 to A.D. 400. The picture that emerges is of early and widespread use and acceptance of 1 John, a growing acceptance of one other letter, if not of two others, and a final universal acceptance of all three. It is time to look at the letters themselves, and to see what they tell us about themselves.

WHAT THE LETTERS ARE ABOUT

We are concerned with three documents, called in the N.E.B. the first, second and third letters of John respectively. We must not assume from these titles that we know for certain that all three letters were written by one man, nor, if they were, that we know who he was or whether he wrote other books also called by the name John—we must look at all that when we come to the question of the authorship of the books. But we can look at the books themselves and see what they are saying, and we can try to picture the situation of those to whom they were addressed.

We can begin by noting that Letter 2 is a summary of Letter 1, and that Letter 3 is a different kind of letter altogether. Letter 1 is the important one, and we will begin by examining that.

I JOHN

The whole of this letter is headed in the N.E.B. 'Recall to fundamentals'. What this title implies is that when the letter was written some time had passed since the Christian gospel had been preached to and received by the recipients of the letter. In the course of the years new ideas had infiltrated into the minds of the readers, and the author is anxious to bring them back into a true appreciation of the main points of the Christian faith. If we see what he is saying we may get some clues as to why he is saying it.

If you read 1 John straight through, you will notice that it is worded for the most part in very *general terms*. It does not refer to particular persons by name, nor to places, nor to events that can be pin-pointed or dated. Apart from a few curious expressions (e.g. 1 John 2: 18, about 'antichrists') most of it could have been written anywhere and at any time. Closer examination, however, will show that it fits a certain historical situation particularly well. That time and place (about A.D. 100 in Asia Minor or Syria) happen to coincide with what we have other reasons for believing to be the true place and time of its appearance.

The letter presents to its readers a series of *tests* whereby their lives, and the lives of other professing Christians, can be judged. Just as in the laboratory we are given a piece of litmus paper and told to judge the acid or alkaline quality of a liquid by seeing how the paper behaves when dipped in the liquid, here we are given several tests which can be applied to our lives in order to see how they stand in relation to the demands and privileges of the Christian faith.

Without attempting here a detailed summary of each chapter we can notice that the letter starts with the fundamental announcement (1: 5—all references till further notice will apply to 1 John, unless otherwise specified) 'God is light'. Even this brief expression needs a good deal of explaining, but for the moment we will assume that it means 'God is all

goodness; there is no place in his Being for anything bad—
for dark deeds or thoughts—or for anything that we would
associate with "the seamy side" of life as we know it'. This
being so, our writer says, or rather assumes, Christian people
should 'walk in the light' (1: 7). There is, however, always
the danger that people who think they are walking in light are
in fact walking in darkness. Much of the letter is an attempt to
show the real tests whereby we can discover whether we are
walking in the light or walking in the dark.

Thus, following 1: 7, two different attitudes to sin are
clearly contrasted. It can be faced, admitted, confessed and
forgiven, or it can be denied or ignored, tolerated and en-
joyed. According as our attitudes fall into one or other of
these two groups we can tell, says the writer, whether we are
walking in light or darkness.

Two different attitudes to our neighbour (or as this book
says our 'brother') can be distinguished—that of love, and
that of hate. Love belongs to light: hate to darkness (1: 9-11;
3: 14, 15; 4: 20, 21, etc.). Here is another test to apply to
human life, and a very revealing one.

Then there is the test of faith—whether or not we believe
rightly about God, and especially about Jesus Christ. There was
a belief in the first century that a great opponent to Christ and
his Church would arise, and this opponent must sometimes have been described as *antichrist* (e.g. 2 Thess. 2: 3, 4,
'...wickedness will be revealed in human form, the man
doomed to perdition. He is the Enemy'). This idea is used by
our writer to characterize opposition to the true faith. The
word is used in the plural (2: 18, 'many antichrists') and
describes those who have taught, or accepted, what is to our
writer a false faith. These men have denied 'both the Father
and the Son' (2: 22). In particular, they have denied 'that
Jesus Christ has come in the flesh' (4: 2).

In the light of all these tests the readers of the letter are
called to examine their lives and attitudes, and at all points to
return to, or adhere to, the original basic fundamentals of the

faith. They are to go back to what 'was there from the beginning' (1: 1). They are to keep to 'the old command' (2: 7).
They are to grasp the one supreme truth that 'the Father sent
the Son to be the saviour of the world' (4: 14). This is the
supreme proof and sign of God's love (4: 9). Our love, for
God and our fellows, is our small response to this love of God
for men (4: 11).

THE SITUATION IN VIEW

It is clear to those who know the religious history of the first
and second centuries A.D. that the situation to which 1 John is
addressed corresponds closely to that produced by the school
of thought called *gnostic* or more precisely *docetic-gnostic*. We
must explain these words.

In the first, and especially in the second Christian century,
we are often made aware of a religious or philosophical
movement which was strongly opposed by the orthodox
Christian teachers like Irenaeus and Tertullian. Its fundamental principle was that matter (the physical world, and the
physical body of man) was evil, and that salvation consisted in
the delivery of the soul or spirit from its bondage in material
things. It had absorbed much of this from the East, the home
of dualism (the belief that two powers, good and evil, were
always at war in the world), but some of its main principles
could be seen in the writings of Plato and other Greeks. It is
now known that this 'gnosticism' had also infiltrated into
Judaism. Traces of it are found for instance in the Dead Sea
Scrolls. It is called *gnosticism* because it laid stress on knowledge (Greek: *gnosis*) as the key by which those who 'knew'
could unlock the prison of matter and escape into the freedom
of the spirit.

Docetism is a kind of gnosticism existing for a time *within*
the Christian Church. Since they believed that matter, including the body, was evil in itself, docetists had difficulty in
believing that 'the Word became flesh' (John 1: 14); so they

9

came to believe that the Son of God did not really *become man*; he only *seemed* to do so (*dokei*—it seems). The divine Christ, it was said, descended on Jesus at his baptism. He did not really die, so they taught. People thought he did, but actually he disappeared or vanished just before the crucifixion, leaving only the human Jesus to suffer and to die. All this is attributed by Irenaeus to a teacher called Cerinthus. His time was about A.D. 100; his home Ephesus. According to Polycarp 'John, the disciple of the Lord' once heard that Cerinthus was in the same bath-house as himself, and fled in terror, 'lest the building should collapse on such an enemy of the truth' (Eusebius, *Ecclesiastical History*, III. 28. 6).

Much of the teaching of our letter can be explained as an answer to this sort of heresy. Against all such beliefs, the author calls his readers back to the old faith, back to what 'was there from the beginning'. They must cling to the belief that Jesus Christ had really 'come in the flesh', that God was then man, completely, and all the time. They must see in this the act of God, and the proof of his love. They must keep the commandment Christ had given, that of mutual love. They must not allow strange ideas about flesh and spirit to lead them into thinking that their human lives, and therefore their moral behaviour, did not matter. If they were really God's children, God's character would be stamped upon them.

This is one main clue that is needed for the understanding of the first letter of John. In the course of his letter, written as we think, to repudiate these gnostic ideas, he throws out many terse summaries of important Christian truths. It is for these, rather than for an answer to gnosticism, that Christians have read his letter for nearly 1900 years, and still read it. The assurances which he gives his readers, the solid foundations on which he tells them to build their hopes, are as relevant today as when they were first written.

There is no clue in the letter to its geographical destination. All the traditions link the writer with Ephesus, but to what particular group in that vicinity or further away the letter was addressed we cannot tell. Its readers were Greek-speaking, but they may well have been Greek-speaking Jews (already converted to Christianity), although this cannot be certainly proved. There is no reference to the Old Testament as an authority, but as the letter is so short, nothing much can be built on that.

2 JOHN

This letter is almost identical with 3 John as far as its length, shape, introduction and conclusion are concerned, but its subject-matter is almost identical with that of 1 John. Like 3 John it claims to come from 'the elder' (verse 1, cf. 3 John 1); like 3 John it ends with disparaging references to correspondence with pen and ink, and with a desire for personal contact. 'Knowing the truth' (verse 1) recalls to mind John 8: 32 'you shall know the truth, and the truth will set you free'. Verse 5 recalls 1 John 2: 7, 'Dear friends, I give you no new command. It is the old command which you always had before you; the old command is the message which you heard at the beginning'. Verse 7 suggests 1 John 2: 22, 'Who is the liar? Who but he that denies that Jesus is the Christ?' and 1 John 4: 2, 3, 'every spirit which acknowledges that Jesus Christ has come in the flesh is from God, and every spirit which does not thus acknowledge Jesus is not from God. This is what is meant by "Antichrist"'. Only one point is really new, that in verse 10, where an order is given not to receive into the home or to greet any travellers who do not teach orthodox doctrine. This presents a complete contrast to the situation in 3 John, addressed to Gaius, who is congratulated on the fact that *he* does receive emissaries from the writer, in contrast with Diotrephes who does not. Of course *these* emissaries are orthodox in belief, or thought to be so by the writer.

The whole letter could be a short summary of 1 John, written to one place at some particular time: it could equally well be a 'first draft', used as the basis of the much longer first letter, which has more the character of a tract or small book. It is addressed to 'the Lady chosen by God, and her children' (verse 1). If we had no other clues, we might think that an individual family was referred to, but the last verse reads as follows: 'The children of your Sister, chosen by God, send their greetings.' This makes it virtually certain that 'the Lady...and her children' means a congregation with its members, and that the greetings come from a sister church with *its* members.

For 'the elder' (verse 1) see below, p. 15.

3 JOHN

This letter, as we have seen, is very similar in form to 2 John. It has the same author (to all appearances), the same length, the same kind of ending. In other ways it is very different. It is addressed to a named individual (Gaius, verse 1—nothing more is known of him). It refers to two others: Diotrephes, (verse 9) and Demetrius (verse 12), both unknown. It describes precise events—the kindness of Gaius to the emissaries of the writer; the refusal of Diotrephes to receive the writer's friends, and his hostility to those who wished to receive them (verses 9, 10); and the reputation of Demetrius (verse 12) who gets good marks, for what exactly we do not know.

When this has been said speculation begins. The natural assumption is that the writer of the letter is head of some church which is sufficiently big (relatively speaking) to send missionaries out and about into the surrounding districts. The local leader of one of the churches on their route, Diotrephes, for some reason objects to the reception of the missionaries. Perhaps he thought them unorthodox, or possibly *too* orthodox (if he himself leaned towards gnosticism). Perhaps he objected to 'the elder' sending missionaries round at all, seeing in this action a claim to a 'district superintendency'— some have called it a claim to the status of an archbishop. Perhaps he disliked the financial and domestic burdens involved in the necessary hospitality. There is not quite enough information to pin-point the situation exactly, but there is given us here a picture of real life in the primitive church, and as there are definite links between this letter and the other Johannine letters and writings, we can imagine the sort of background against which the other writings are to be placed.

The exact points of controversy are not stated, but verse 11 ('The well-doer is a child of God; the evil-doer has never seen God') links up closely with 1 John 2: 29 and 1 John 3: 6. Both writings have in mind circles where people claimed to have 'seen God' but showed little regard in life for the claims of Christian morality. If you believe that the flesh is evil, you are not surprised or worried if people act evilly, and you may feel at liberty to act evilly too.

THE RELATION OF THE JOHANNINE WRITINGS TO EACH OTHER, AND PROBLEMS OF THEIR AUTHORSHIP

We cannot postpone any longer looking at the difficult question of the relation of our three letters to each other, and to two other books commonly associated with the name 'John'—the Fourth Gospel and the Revelation of John—the last book of the Bible.

For many hundreds of years—shall we say from A.D. 400 till 1800, and in some circles till much later—it was assumed that all five writings came from the pen of John, the son of Zebedee, disciple and apostle of Jesus, thought to have survived to a great age, to have lived in Ephesus, and at one time to have been imprisoned or exiled for his faith to Patmos, an island in the Aegean Sea. In the last hundred years or so it has come to be seen that every point in this general group of interrelated beliefs is open to question, although the answers to the questions raised are almost as numerous as the scholars who have raised them.

All the important 'external evidence' (information about the books outside the books themselves) goes back to Irenaeus,

the theological teacher of the last quarter of the second century
to whom we have already referred. He came to the West
from the East, and claims to have heard Polycarp, who lived
from say A.D. 69 till A.D. 155 and was bishop of Smyrna.
Irenaeus speaks quite clearly of his contacts with Polycarp in
his own boyhood, and claims that he had heard from Polycarp of that veteran saint's contact with 'John and with the
others who had seen the Lord' (Eusebius, *History*, v. 20. 4–8).
Irenaeus does not state that his opinion that John lived a long
time and wrote the Gospel came from Polycarp, but it is a
not unnatural deduction from what he does say. With our
increasing knowledge of different views held in ancient times
(including the view that John the Apostle suffered an early
martyrdom with James his brother, who was beheaded by
Herod Agrippa I in A.D. 44: see Acts 12: 2) we cannot accept
Irenaeus's conclusions without examining the internal evidence
for ourselves. We must now turn to that task.

Let us first make a list of unquestioned facts and then see into
what coherent patterns they can be woven.

(1) The only book of these five in which the author's name
is said to be 'John' is Revelation (Rev. 1: 1, 4),

(2) Two books claim to come from 'the elder' (2 John 1;
3 John 1).

(3) There are other close similarities between 2 John and
3 John.

(4) There are close similarities in subject-matter between
2 John and 1 John.

(5) There are a vast number of close similarities of idea,
phrasing and vocabulary between the Gospel and the letters.

(6) There are a few similarities, but great differences, between Revelation and all the other writings under consideration.

(7) The Gospel is in some way related—or so it claims—to
the Beloved Disciple—'the disciple whom Jesus loved'. At
John 21: 24 there is a claim that that disciple 'wrote' the stories
there recorded. Whether it was intended to claim his author-

ship for the whole Gospel, or only for what we call chapter 21, is uncertain. By 'the disciple whom Jesus loved' it is probable, though not quite certain, that John, the son of Zebedee, is intended.

Now as we saw at the beginning of this section, tradition has put all these facts together and drawn the conclusion (in the opinion of most modern scholars, wrongly) that there is one author for all five books, and that that author is John the son of Zebedee.

We must now take note of the *general* opinion of modern scholarship on these matters. To explain how this opinion has been arrived at would be too great a task for a commentary of this size. Everybody, however, who studies the letters (and the other Johannine books) can have these ideas at the back of his mind, and decide how far they are supported or challenged by the evidence he sees.

Most modern scholars find it impossible to believe that all or any of these books were written by John the son of Zebedee (though some would allow his claim to have written Revelation).

Many would accept 'the elder' as the author of the three letters and the Gospel. They would connect this shadowy personage with a person described in the writings of Papias as 'the elder John' (not of course 'the older of two Johns' but a person known as the elder—the 'senior member'—John). Papias refers to 'the elder John' *after* referring to John among the main list of the apostles. Possibly those who had known and worked with apostles were called elders.

The general (though not universal) opinion of scholars is in favour of one author for the Gospel and the letters and a different one for Revelation. This is because the style and language of the Gospel and letters are extraordinarily similar, while the language of Revelation is quite different. The subject-matter of the latter, with all its strange visions of the supernatural world, is altogether different from the 'spiritual' subject-matter of the Gospel and letters. One further point perhaps deserves mention. The view has recently been expressed that the prologue to the Gospel (John 1: 1–14) and the epilogue (John 21) may have been added to the Gospel a good deal after the original writing of that book. According to this view they bear a closer relationship to the letters than the rest of the Gospel, and the order of writing may have been (1) the main part of the Gospel (2) the letters (3) the prologue and epilogue to the Gospel.

The area in which all or any of these books originated has also been the subject of scholarly inquiry. Revelation, with its seven letters to seven Asiatic churches, ties itself to Asia (what we should now call Turkey—the old Asia Minor). Tradition ties John to Ephesus. The Gospel and letters may well have originated in or near Ephesus. Claims have, however, been made for Syria (Ignatius, bishop of Antioch *c.* A.D. 115, writes in his letters in a way reminiscent of John) and also for Alexandria. Almost anywhere where Greek was spoken, and the story of Jesus loved and relied upon, would do.

✶ ✶ ✶ ✶ ✶ ✶ ✶ ✶ ✶ ✶ ✶ ✶ ✶

THE FIRST LETTER OF JOHN

Recall to Fundamentals

THE PROLOGUE

1 IT WAS THERE from the beginning; we have heard it; we have seen it with our own eyes; we looked upon it, and felt it with our own hands; and it is of this we tell.

2 Our theme is the word of life. This life was made visible; we have seen it and bear our testimony; we here declare to you the eternal life which dwelt with the Father and

3 was made visible to us. What we have seen and heard we

declare to you, so that you and we together may share in
a common life, that life which we share with the Father
and his Son Jesus Christ. And we write this in order that 4
the joy of us all may be complete.

✻ What was there from the beginning? That is not an easy
question to answer, and the N.E.B. has made the sentence
look rather more straightforward than it is in the original
Greek. The Greek (and in this particular sentence it is important to start from the original language) says something like
this: 'The thing that was there from the start, the thing that we
have heard, seen with our eyes, gazed at, that our hands felt, concerning the message of life—and the life was made visible...'
(from there onwards the N.E.B. gives a clear translation).

Verse 3 really summarizes the whole prologue—*What we
have seen and heard we declare to you.* Reading backwards we
find that what was declared by the writer was (verse 2) *the
eternal life which dwelt with the Father and was made visible to us.*
This clearly refers to the life of Jesus Christ, which the writer
accepts as an unveiling of the eternal life of God. *This life was
made visible* (verse 2). As the whole book is about this revelation of God in Jesus Christ, the writer can truly say (verse 2),
Our theme is the word (the message) *of life.* Now we can see the
significance of the series of statements at the beginning of the
section. This revelation was *there from the beginning.* There is
little doubt that *the beginning* here means 'from the earliest
stage of the Christian Church'. The vivid words *heard, seen it,
looked upon it, felt it,* seem to suggest the vivid contacts of the
first disciples with Jesus himself. As, however, it is unlikely
that these words were written by an actual disciple, we must
assume that the *we* of verse 1 and later verses means 'all of us
Christians'. Some of them were actually there 'from the
beginning'. Others had entered into their heritage.

The writer is laying down his theme at the very start;
Christianity has to do with an actual historical manifestation.
The eternal, essential life of God had been shown in Jesus.

This passage has some links with the opening section of the Fourth Gospel (John 1: 1–14). There too we have the phrase 'at the beginning'; there we read of 'the Word'—meaning there the Eternal Son of God (see John 1: 14); there we have the same vivid sense of an earthly unveiling of a divine life (for this, see also John 1: 14).

The purpose behind the writing of the book is to enable the readers to share fully in the life of the believing community, a life which is itself a sharing in the eternal life of the Father and the Son (verse 3). The shared life leads to a completed joy (verse 4). As is seen in the Fourth Gospel (John 15: 11), the sharing of truth and life leads to fullness of life, and to the fullness of joy.

That is a short prologue to the whole book, a kind of over-ture to the symphony. Many of these themes will occur again, especially that of the reality of the Incarnation (the coming of the Son of God in real humanity, in *flesh*) and of the reality of the Christian's fellowship with God through faith in, and obedience to, Christ, his Son. ✶

WALKING IN THE LIGHT

5 Here is the message we heard from him and pass on to you: that God is light, and in him there is no darkness at
6 all. If we claim to be sharing in his life while we walk in
7 the dark, our words and our lives are a lie; but if we walk in the light as he himself is in the light, then we share together a common life, and we are being cleansed from every sin by the blood of Jesus his Son.

8 If we claim to be sinless, we are self-deceived and
9 strangers to the truth. If we confess our sins, he is just, and may be trusted to forgive our sins and cleanse us from
10 every kind of wrong; but if we say we have committed no sin, we make him out to be a liar, and then his word has no place in us.

My children, in writing thus to you my purpose is that **2**
you should not commit sin. But should anyone commit
a sin, we have one to plead our cause with the Father,
Jesus Christ, and he is just. He is himself the remedy for 2
the defilement of our sins, not our sins only but the sins of
all the world.

Here is the test by which we can make sure that we 3
know him: do we keep his commands? The man who 4
says, 'I know him', while he disobeys his commands, is a
liar and a stranger to the truth; but in the man who is 5
obedient to his word, the divine love has indeed come to
its perfection.

✻ This passage opens up one of the main themes of the letter
—what are the reliable signs of a life really lived in fellowship
with God? It is a mistake, in reading this book, to look for an
exact logical argument, either in the whole book, or in each
section. When the writer wants to explore and expose a certain truth he does not lay it out as an architect might lay out a
plan of a building. His habit is to look at a truth from many
points of view—rather like a man strolling round the outside,
and then the inside of an old church. Each verse often repeats
what was said before, but with a slightly different point
emphasized.

Here we begin with an important statement (verse 5): *God
is light*. This message, he says, they had heard *from him* and
there can be little doubt that the *him* means Jesus. Actually
nowhere in the Gospels do we read any words very like these.
We do of course find constant references to light and darkness, e.g. Matt. 5: 14, 'You are light for all the world', and
there are many such references in the Fourth Gospel, e.g.
John 1: 4, 5, 'that life was the light of men. The light shines on
in the dark, and the darkness has never quenched it.' Or again,
John 8: 12, where Jesus says 'I am the light of the world. No

follower of mine shall wander in the dark.' So as Jesus was thought to be the visible image of God the Father (see John 14: 9, 'anyone who has seen me has seen the Father'), it was not a long step to take to say that Jesus' message was *God is light*.

In using this expression, however, the writer was being very bold, and taking a phrase used by the school of thought he was opposing. Philo, a Greek-writing Jewish scholar of Alexandria, about contemporary with Jesus, uses the actual words 'God is light' (*De Somniis*, I, 75). The Hermetic literature (mystical books in Greek and Latin, claiming to come from 'Hermes the thrice-greatest', roughly dating from the first four Christian centuries) uses similar expressions. The Dead Sea Scrolls make frequent use of the contrast between light and darkness as symbolic of the conflict between God's true people and his enemies. This is seen in the scroll entitled *The War of the Sons of Light and the Sons of Darkness*, and also *The Manual of Discipline*, where some sentences come very close to our writer's words in verses 6 and 7. See, for example, *Manual*, III, 'All who practise righteousness are under the domination of the Prince of Light, and walk in the ways of light; whereas all who practise perversity are under the domination of the Angel of Darkness and walk in the ways of darkness'. Our writer is not afraid to use similar expressions, but shows by the way he uses them that 'light and darkness' mean to him 'good and evil'—moral goodness, and moral badness. When he says (verse 5) *in him there is no darkness at all* he means God is all goodness, or pictorially, all light.

If therefore our lives are bad, if we are 'walking in the dark' (verse 6), and if we claim to be sharing God's life, we are on a thoroughly false foundation—the words are untrue, and the deeds are deceptive. If, on the other hand, we *walk in the light* (verse 7) we are indeed sharing the common life that belongs to Christians, a life of fellowship with God and with other Christians, and the process of our being cleansed from all our sins is going forward (verse 7, end). This cleansing is *by the blood of Jesus his Son.* In the Jewish sacrifices the blood of the animal was felt to represent *its life*, and when the blood was spilt in sacrifice (Lev. 17: 11) cleansing of or atonement for sin could take place. Our writer says that the death of Jesus worked in this way. His 'blood', his life offered in death, was powerfully working in the Christian community, cleansing from sin those who had their faces to the light.

The important thing was to admit and confess sin (verses 8–10). It was only self-deception to claim to be sinless, or never to have committed sin. Forgiveness from sin's guilt, and delivery from its power, could be confidently looked for from God if honest confession was made (verse 9).

At the beginning of chapter 2, the author makes it plain that he is not condoning or ignoring sin—his purpose in writing (2: 1) is to prevent them falling into sin. But sin will nevertheless trip them up (in spite of 3: 9 which we shall consider later). When this happens they must know that they have one to 'plead their cause with the Father'. The word translated *one to plead our cause* ('advocate' in the N.E.B. footnote) is the Greek word *paraklētos*. This means 'one called in to help', usually an advocate in a law-court. This word is used for the Holy Spirit in the Gospel—'another Comforter' in the old versions of the Bible (see John 14: 15, 16; 15: 26, etc.) and 'your Advocate' in the N.E.B. Here the meaning is clear. Jesus, righteous himself, and the answer to the sins of those who trust him, stands before his Father fully accepted by God. His perfection, and especially his perfect self-offering of himself, avail to cover, or wipe away, the sins of those who are united with him in faith and trust. The Greek word *hilasmos* here translated as 'the remedy for the defilement' (verse 2), used to be translated as 'propitiation', and was thought to stand for the process whereby an angry God was made friendly or *propitious*. For many years it has been known that in Hebrew thought God himself was 'the cleanser', the forgiver. It was the sins that had to be cleansed, not the Holy God persuaded to overlook them. This discovery lies behind the N.E.B.

rendering of 2: 2. Notice also that this cleansing process is intended to operate for all humanity (2: 2; cf. John 11: 51, 52, 'he was prophesying that Jesus would die for the nation—die not for the nation alone but to gather together the scattered children of God').

2: 3–5 is really making the same point over again. The claim here tested is contained in the words 'I know him' (verse 4). This may have been frequently on the lips of the 'knowers', the gnostics. We are taught that this claim too stands or falls with the *obedience* of the claimant to the commands of God. The idea of the love of God coming to perfection in the good Christian (verse 5) is twice used by Clement, writing from Rome to Corinth about A.D. 96. It would be interesting to know if he had read our book, or if our author had read his letter, but the words used are too brief to make certain any such deduction. ✳

ANOTHER TEST: LIVING LIKE CHRIST

Here is the test by which we can make sure that we are
6 in him: whoever claims to be dwelling in him, binds
7 himself to live as Christ himself lived. Dear friends, I give
you no new command. It is the old command which you
always had before you; the old command is the message
8 which you heard at the beginning. And yet again it is
a new command that I am giving you—new in the sense
that the darkness is passing and the real light already shines.
Christ has made this true, and it is true in your own
experience.

✳ The test now offered is said to be a test by which we can be sure *that we are in him* (verse 5). *Him* means Jesus Christ, and to be 'in him' means to be united with him, to belong to him, to trust in him, to be one of his true disciples. The phrase is similar to that in John 15: 4, where Jesus says 'Dwell in me, as I in you. No branch can bear fruit by itself, but only if it remains united with the vine; no more can you bear fruit, unless you remain united with me'. (We may notice how in translating this passage, the N.E.B. translators have used the phrase 'united with me' as a variant to 'dwell in me', much as we have done earlier in this note.) Those who are *in him* in this sense must follow his example, 'walk as he walked' (to use for once the language of the Authorized and Revised Versions of verse 6, certainly closer to the Greek and its Hebrew equivalents, than the N.E.B.), to live as he lived. When the N.E.B. says *Christ himself* in verse 6, it is translating the Greek word *ekeinos*—he, 'that man there'—which is used frequently in the letter for Christ (3: 3, 5, 7, 16 and 4: 17). There are some similar, but not identical, uses in the Gospel (e.g. John 3: 30, '*he* [*ekeinos*] grows greater'; John 9: 37, 'it is *he* [*ekeinos*] who is speaking to you'). The importance of following, i.e. copying or imitating Christ, is prominent in the New Testament, e.g. John 13: 15, 'I have set you an example: you are to do as I have done for you' and 1 Pet. 2: 21, 'Christ...left you an example; it is for you to follow in his steps'.

There follow some rather curious statements about the command that is being given. It is first described (verse 7) as *no new command*. Then as *the old command* (verse 7). Then in verse 8, as *a new command*. The train of thought is this: as they have to copy, or follow Christ, it is clear that they are not being set some new or novel task. No, it is the same old command that Christians have always had to obey. Yet, in another sense, it is a new command, in the sense that every aspect of the Christian life is *new*. It belongs to the new age, the age (verse 8) in which the darkness is passing away, and the real light—the light of God in Christ—is shining. We at once recall John 1: 5, 'The light shines on in the dark' and John 1: 9, 'The real light which enlightens every man was even then coming into the world'. The passage ends with a cryptic saying, *Christ has made this true, and it is true in your own experience* (verse 8). The translators of the N.E.B. have given a precise meaning to a phrase which in the Greek is rather vague and general. The literal translation is: 'I write a new command to you—which is true in him and in you.' The N.E.B. has probably guessed the right meaning of this mysterious phrase, but another meaning might well be 'this newness belongs to the life and work of Christ, and you Christians share it'. The N.E.B. has been able to emphasize the word 'true', but *Christ has made this true* is not clearly represented in the original. ✳

YET ANOTHER TEST: LOVING YOUR 'BROTHER'

9 A man may say, 'I am in the light'; but if he hates his
10 brother, he is still in the dark. Only the man who loves his brother dwells in light: there is nothing to make him
11 stumble. But one who hates his brother is in darkness; he walks in the dark and has no idea where he is going, because the darkness has made him blind.

✳ This passage is the continuation of the preceding one. There the claim was to be 'dwelling in him' (verse 6); here it is to be *in the light* (verse 9). We have already come across this idea of being 'in the light' in 1: 7. There to 'walk in the light' was put before the readers as a positive ideal. Here we are concerned with those who claim, rather superficially, to be *in the light*, to be in touch with God, to have the special saving knowledge. Our writer says that the presence of hatred in the heart (for a brother—he would possibly include any neighbour under this title in this context, but see pp. 41, 51–3) is a sure sign that the person thus hating is in the dark. To the writer, God is both love and light. Not to share God's love means not to share his light. If love means light, hate means darkness. The man who loves his brother is dwelling in the light; therefore he is not likely to run into something that will trip him up, something *to make him stumble* (verse 10).

The writer may well have meant 'stumbling-blocks are not present *in the light*'. We all know that hatred warps the judgement and leads to many other sins. Verse 11 repeats the same thought, with the extension that the walker-in-the-dark does not know where he is going. He is like a blind man (verse 11). ✻

WHY THE LETTER IS BEING WRITTEN

I write to you, my children, because your sins have been 12
    forgiven for his sake.

I write to you, fathers, because you know him who is and 13
    has been from the beginning.

I write to you, young men, because you have mastered
    the evil one.

To you, children, I have written because you know the
    Father.

To you, fathers, I have written because you know him 14
    who is and has been from the beginning.

To you, young men, I have written because you are
    strong; God's word is in you, and you have mastered
    the evil one.

✻ Here we come to a curious parenthesis, in which the author gives his reasons for addressing various groups among his readers. The whole passage is printed in the N.E.B. rather like blank verse. There is a repetitive rhythm in the original Greek, but whether the author was aware of any change from prose to poetry is doubtful.

Notice some 'structural' points in this extract. There are three sentences in each group of sayings. The first three begin *I write* (present tense); the second, *I have written*. Although different tenses are used in the Greek (present and aorist—our 'past definite') the writer probably intended no distinction.

Greek could use what was known as *epistolary aorist*, a past tense originating from the fact that by the time the letter was read the past tense would be appropriate. Then notice that the three groupings run 'children, fathers, young men' in each triplet of sayings. Probably *children* (or more accurately, *my children*) in verses 12 and 13 *b* includes *all* the readers, his children in the faith or in the Church. Elsewhere he addresses all his readers like this (2: 28; 3: 18; 4: 4). Then he seems to divide up his audience into old and young—'fathers' and 'young men'. The absence of any feminine classification reflects the 'all-male' nature of the deliberating, governing part of the primitive Christian congregations. It is tempting to feel that only *one* set of three address-sentences was meant to stay in the letter. Possibly the second group of three sentences was meant as a better version of the first three, and the writer forgot to cross the first three out!

A few words are needed about the reasons given for addressing each group.

The children—probably the whole audience, as we saw—are addressed (verses 12 and 13 *b*) because their 'sins have been forgiven' and because they 'know the Father'. Both experiences are closely connected with the *start* of the Christian life. Baptism leads to forgiveness (Acts 2: 38, '"Repent," said Peter, "repent and be baptized, every one of you, in the name of Jesus the Messiah for the forgiveness of your sins"') and to the acknowledgement of God as Father (Gal. 4: 6, 7, 'God has sent into our hearts the Spirit of his Son, crying "Abba! Father!"'). Fathers are said in both triplets (groups of three verses) to 'know him who is and has been from the beginning' —as if the writer meant that their age, or long-standing in the Church, ensured that they knew the Lord who had ruled the Church since its founding. There *could* be a reference to the existence of Christ as the *eternal* Word, or Son of God, but such knowledge does not belong particularly to the seniors in the Church. Young men are said to have mastered the evil one, and in one clause to 'be strong'. It could be said that the presence of the young men in the Christian community, at the time when their passions and appetites were at their height, was a proof that they had, in some measure, overcome the evil one. But all the individual attributes of the groups overlap, and it is probably true that the writer is just 'reacting' to associations in his own mind as he describes his readers in this way. 'His children' bring to his mind their entry into the Christian family; 'fathers' suggests antiquity, the faith that went back to the beginning; young men, strength, first physical, and then by analogy, spiritual. ✶

'THE GODLESS WORLD'

Do not set your hearts on the godless world or anything 15 in it. Anyone who loves the world is a stranger to the Father's love. Everything the world affords, all that 16 panders to the appetites, or entices the eyes, all the glamour of its life, springs not from the Father but from the godless world. And that world is passing away with 17 all its allurements, but he who does God's will stands for evermore.

✶ Having allowed himself a little parenthesis on his grounds for addressing them, the writer returns to his work of teaching and guiding his readers. Here he tells them what attitude they should adopt to the world they live in, in certain of its aspects. As these few verses are among the most difficult for a modern Christian (especially a modern *young* Christian) to accept, we must be very careful to understand exactly what is being said.

First let us try to grasp what the writer meant to say to his contemporary readers.

To begin with, it must be said that the word 'godless' does not appear in the original Greek as an adjective qualifying the word 'world'. What the Greek actually says is (to quote the Authorized and Revised Versions) 'Love not the world'. The

N.E.B. translators have decided that here 'the world' means 'the world on its worst side'—the world organized, as it largely is, without reference to God and his will, or without that true knowledge of him that Jesus Christ gives. The Fourth Gospel uses the word 'world' to describe 'mankind' or all humanity. In this sense, its author can say (John 3: 16) 'God loved the world so much that he gave his only Son'—the implication being that though the world needed saving, it was worth saving. This statement is closely paralleled in our book at 4: 9, 'his love was disclosed to us in this, that he sent his only Son into the world to bring us life'. Similarly at 4: 14 we learn that 'the Father sent the Son to be the saviour of the world'. In the Gospel, however, at John 12: 31, the world is a bad world—'Now is the hour of judgement for this world; now shall the Prince of this world be driven out'. Other writers (e.g. Paul) speak of 'this passing age' (1 Cor. 2: 6) rather than 'this world'.

The last verse of the present section (verse 17) shows that the author is not far removed from Paul in thinking of the world as belonging to a temporary, passing, age: *that world is passing away with all its allurements*. He believed that the new age had begun—at least it had begun for those who had been made part of it—*the darkness is passing and the real light already shines* (verse 8). The question then arose as to how the Christian was to behave in the world from which he was inwardly delivered, but in which, at least externally, he still had to live his life. The dilemma is clearly reflected in the prayer of Jesus recorded in John 17, when in verses 13–19 the position of Christians in the world is specifically mentioned. There it is said that 'the world hates them because they are strangers in the world' (verse 14): 'I pray thee', Jesus says, 'not to take them out of the world, but to keep them from the evil one' (verse 15). A similar distinction between going out of the world altogether, and keeping clear of its moral infection is seen in 1 Cor. 5: 9–11.

In our passage, the writer puts his point very starkly. He sees his readers confronted with a direct choice: either they must love the world and the things in it, or the Father: they cannot love both (verse 15). He then gives us a clear picture of the sort of thing he has in mind—it is what *panders to the appetites, or entices the eyes, all the glamour of its life* (verse 16). He can see his readers living perhaps in the gay and exciting city of Ephesus. All around them are the allurements of a life of passionate excitement, of captivating theatrical displays, of boasting competition for earthly fame or wealth. He calls on them to see the transient nature of all this, and instead, to concentrate on obedience to God's will, which has the promise of eternal life.

Now we must think how this applies in modern life. At different times in history, various groups—monks, puritans, modern sects of all kinds—have worked out their particular brand of separation from the world. That all Christians must be *ready* for sacrifice in order to fulfil their vocation, or to safeguard themselves and others from dangerous temptations, is always true. But no one could base his *whole* life on a biblical saying that was very relevant once, may always become relevant, but which nevertheless does not cover the whole situation. There are many things in 'the world' which it is surely right to 'love'—flowers, the stars, the birds, our friends and relations, to mention only a few. God has made us as we are, with eyes and ears to respond to beautiful sights and sounds, and with our sexual natures crying out for satisfaction at the right time and place. What we have to remember is that however bad 'the world' may be it is still God's world. We have to love what is good in it, and hate what is bad. Such discretion is much harder than just accepting the world as we find it, or flying from it in fear or righteous indignation. *

WHERE TRUE KNOWLEDGE LIES

My children, this is the last hour! You were told that 18 Antichrist was to come, and now many antichrists have appeared; which proves to us that this is indeed the last

19 hour. They went out from our company, but never really belonged to us; if they had, they would have stayed with us. They went out, so that it might be clear that not all in our company truly belong to it.

20 You, no less than they, are among the initiated; this is the gift of the Holy One, and by it you all have know-
21 ledge. It is not because you are ignorant of the truth that I have written to you, but because you know it, and because lies, one and all, are alien to the truth.

✻ In this section the writer asserts that a certain division which has occurred in the Church has a deep significance. It indicates in fact that *the last hour* has come—the history of the world, he meant, was about to be drawn to a close. The phrase 'the last day' occurs several times in the Gospel (e.g. John 11: 24). Elsewhere we read of 'the last days' (Acts 2: 17), 'the end of time' (literally 'the last season', 1 Pet. 1: 5), 'the final age' (literally 'the last time', Jude 18). *The last hour* is a phrase special to our letters, but its meaning is similar to all the other phrases mentioned. The author was mistaken as far as his actual assertion was concerned; the world's story has gone on. But there is an ultimate importance about *the truth* and our attitude to it, and in this sense the message about Jesus brings us up against final realities.

They were evidently expecting some striking enemy of Christ to appear (verse 18: 'You were told that Antichrist was to come'). The word *Antichrist* is special to these books, but the idea was to be found in the Old Testament, and it crops up here and there in the New. According to Mark 13: 14, Jesus himself referred to some terrible act of blasphemy that was to come ('"the abomination of desolation", usurping a place which is not his'). St Paul had a similar thought (2 Thess. 2: 3, 4, 'wickedness will be revealed in human form, the man doomed to perdition. He is the Enemy'; 2 Thess. 2: 8, 'then he will be revealed, that wicked man'). All these ideas go back to a Jewish expectation of a 'final fling' by the powers of evil before they are defeated (see, e.g. Daniel 12: 11). Our writer sees in the break-away of the false teachers—those who *went out* because they *never really belonged* (19)—a fulfilment of this expectation. He cannot conceive of anything worse than apparently true believers setting off on a mission to spread what is to him false belief. This point is to be made again in different words in verse 22, in 4: 1–3, and in 2 John 7.

The end of verse 19 means that an inevitable result of their separation was clear evidence that they were not really part of the true company at all. They did not of course secede for this *purpose*, but their secession had that result.

Verses 20 and 21 suggest that some among the readers had a kind of inferiority complex, and wondered whether it was the seceders who really had the truth. So the writer tells them that they too have had a real *anointing*. The Greek word is *chrisma*, the act or material of anointing. ('Christ' comes from *christos*, anointed). In verse 27 there are different versions of a Greek word in a sentence similar to verse 20, *charisma* (gift) appearing in one manuscript instead of *chrisma* (anointing). The N.E.B. translators seem to have interpreted verse 20 by verse 27, and refer here to *the gift of the Holy One*, though they retain the idea of anointing in the phrase *You...are among the initiated*. The important phrase is *you all have knowledge*. Those who seceded doubtless claimed to be 'the knowing ones', the gnostics, but the writer assures his readers that this is not so. He is writing to them (verse 21) because he is sure the truth will find an echo in their hearts. ✶

WHERE REAL ERROR LIES

Who is the liar? Who but he that denies that Jesus is the 22 Christ? He is Antichrist, for he denies both the Father and the Son: to deny the Son is to be without the Father; 23 to acknowledge the Son is to have the Father too. You 24

therefore must keep in your hearts that which you heard
at the beginning; if what you heard then still dwells in
you, you will yourselves dwell in the Son and also in the
25 Father. And this is the promise that he himself gave us,
the promise of eternal life.

✳ Having raised the subject of truth and lying, the writer
now makes quite plain what he thinks is the supreme lie—
it is to deny that Jesus is the Christ. Put in this form it might
seem to be a denial that Jesus was the promised 'Messiah' or
'Anointed one', the fulfilment of Jewish hopes. But a glance
at 4: 2, 3 shows that there are other aspects of the error he
wishes to combat. It is necessary to believe, for instance, that
'Jesus Christ has come in the flesh', that the actual man Jesus,
a real man, was the vehicle of the Divine Presence. This is just
what the docetists and gnostics found so difficult (see pp. 9–11).

Only if they believed in *the Son* in the fullest sense, he says,
could they *have the Father*. The whole of the Johannine literature, Gospel and letters, starts from this relationship between
'the Son' and 'the Father'. Jesus, in his whole life, character,
and work, and especially in his death, is so truly 'his Father's
Son', that to know him is to know God. The key passage
is John 14: 7–11, especially verse 9, 'Anyone who has seen me
has seen the Father'. The essential thing therefore was for them
to cling to the basic gospel which they heard when they became Christians 'at the beginning'. If the message was clung to
faithfully, their own position, *in the Son* and *in the Father*, would
be secure, not otherwise. This position is one which carries
with it the promise of eternal life (verse 25, cf. John 3: 16). ✳

SUMMARY OF LAST TWO SECTIONS

26,27 So much for those who would mislead you. But as for
you, the initiation which you received from him stays
with you; you need no other teacher, but learn all you

need to know from his initiation, which is real and no
illusion. As he taught you, then, dwell in him.

✻ This paragraph adds hardly anything to what has just been
said, but it recapitulates the main points of recent paragraphs.
The author impresses on them the fact that they really have an
anointing, an *initiation*, to use the N.E.B. word. They had
certainly been washed with water, at baptism, but anointing
is not quite the word for that. There *may* have been an actual
anointing with oil, as part of the initiation ceremony. (In
Jas. 5: 14 we read of anointing with oil in connexion with the
healing ministry for the sick.) They certainly looked on the
gift of the Holy Spirit as a kind of anointing (Act 10: 38, for the
anointing of Jesus with the Holy Spirit which follows immediately a reference to 'the baptism proclaimed by John'; 2 Cor.
1: 21, 22, for the anointing of Christians with the Holy
Spirit). In 1 John, whatever outward ceremony may have
been in the background of the writer's mind, he thinks especially of the *teaching* they have received as the supreme gift.
They need no new teacher. To cling to what they were taught
was to have the secret of unbroken fellowship with Christ,
the source and subject of the teaching. ✻

A HOPE WITH A MORAL CHALLENGE

Even now, my children, dwell in him, so that when he 28
appears we may be confident and unashamed before him
at his coming. If you know that he is righteous, you must 29
recognize that every man who does right is his child.
How great is the love that the Father has shown to us! 3
We were called God's children, and such we are; and the
reason why the godless world does not recognize us is that
it has not known him. Here and now, dear friends, we 2
are God's children; what we shall be has not yet been disclosed, but we know that when it is disclosed we shall be

3 like him, because we shall see him as he is. Everyone who
has this hope before him purifies himself, as Christ is pure.

✽ As so often, the author repeats a phrase from the end of one
section, and makes it the starting-point of a new one. Here
the bridge phrase is *dwell in him* (2: 27 and 2: 28). The
essential point of this section is that true followers of Christ
must stick to their faith (to use other language) so that they
may be ready to welcome Christ with confidence, without
embarrassment, *at his coming* (verse 28). The word translated
coming is the Greek word *parousia*, which is used in the Gospels
and in various letters for the 'second' or final appearance of
Christ at the end of time (see, e.g. Matt. 24: 3; 1 Thess. 2: 19).
It really means 'presence', 'being near', but it had a technical
sense in the ancient world, and was used especially of an
arrival of a king on a state visit. This paragraph begins and ends
with the thought that Christians must be ready for their Lord,
and that readiness means *goodness*, being like him in character
(see especially 3: 3).

One or two other important strands of thought are woven
around this main thought. There is the point for instance of
verse 29 that right action is the sure sign of sonship to a
Righteous Father. The 'he' and 'his' of verse 29 are ambiguous. In the phrase *he is righteous* he certainly means Christ,
and carries on naturally from the *his* of *his coming* in verse 28.
But *his child* at the end of verse 29 would seem to mean the
child of *God*. The writer is frequently talking of being 'born
of God', never of being 'born of Christ'. He has made a
jump in his thinking. The sequence in his mind was perhaps
this: Christ is righteous; Christ is the Son of God therefore
God is righteous; righteous men must be God's children, for
it is always a case of 'like father, like son'. We might have
expected the writer to say 'every child of God does right'.
Actually he says 'Everyone who does right is God's child'. If
we could have heard him *say* the words (and pretending for
the moment that he spoke English), he perhaps said 'every

man who *does* right is his child', stressing the doing rather than the all-inclusiveness of the 'every man'.

The thought of our being sons of God causes the outburst of praise in 3: 1, *How great is the love that the Father has shown to us!* To be called God's children (verse 1) is indeed an incalculable benefit, but he adds *and such we are*—it is not only a matter of names and titles; it is a solid reality. The world in general does not see this, but after all, the writer says, *it has not known him.* As we read in John 1, 'the world...did not recognize him. He entered his own realm, and his own would not receive him' (John 1: 10, 11). Even this wonderful experience, that of being God's children, is only a beginning; *what we shall be has not yet been disclosed* (verse 2). The future holds the promise that *we shall see him as he is* (verse 2). He believes that this carries with it the certainty *that we shall be like him.* Why exactly this should be so is not made clear but the general teaching of the Bible is that it is only the pure in heart who see God in his full purity and glory (see Matt. 5: 8). So to our writer the converse is true; those who see God will be made clean and pure. Here is the incentive to begin the process of becoming more like God in purity of character (verse 3). ✳

SIN IS NOT FOR CHRISTIANS

To commit sin is to break God's law: sin, in fact, is lawless- 4
ness. Christ appeared, as you know, to do away with sins, 5
and there is no sin in him. No man therefore who dwells 6
in him is a sinner; the sinner has not seen him and does
not know him.

My children, do not be misled: it is the man who does 7
right who is righteous, as God is righteous; the man who 8
sins is a child of the devil, for the devil has been a sinner
from the first; and the Son of God appeared for the very
purpose of undoing the devil's work.

9   A child of God does not commit sin, because the divine
     seed remains in him; he cannot be a sinner, because he is
10   God's child. That is the distinction between the children
     of God and the children of the devil: no one who does not
     do right is God's child, nor is anyone who does not love
11   his brother. For the message you have heard from the
12   beginning is this: that we should love one another; unlike
     Cain, who was a child of the evil one and murdered his
     brother. And why did he murder him? Because his own
     actions were wrong, and his brother's were right.

* These three paragraphs are really saying the same thing
three times over, with a slightly different emphasis or 'slant'
each time. The thing they say in common is this: Christians
must turn their backs on sin. Sin cannot be entertained as in
any way compatible with claiming to be a Christian, a follower
or 'a member' of Christ.

The first paragraph (verses 4–6) makes this point in this way:
Christians live ('dwell') in Christ; they have seen him, with
the eye of faith; they know him (verse 6). But there is no sin
in Christ (an early example of the doctrine of the sinlessness of
Christ—verse 5). On the other hand his appearance in the
world was expressly for the purpose of abolishing sin (verse 5).
This corresponds with what is said in the Gospel (John 1: 29,
'The next day he saw Jesus coming towards him. "Look," he
said, "there is the Lamb of God; it is he who takes away the
sin of the world"'). Sin, we are told, is breaking God's law.
Here the content of God's law is not defined, still less defended.
It is assumed that Christian people know well enough the
main outline of God's law of behaviour. It will be noticed
that this paragraph has been explained 'from the bottom up',
or from the end back to the beginning. This is often useful in
understanding this letter. If you see where the writer arrives
at the end, it is often possible to trace his line of thought, with
its intermediate steps.

The second paragraph (verses 7 and 8) puts the same point from a slightly different angle. It emphasizes the positive, rather than the negative, aspect of the realities of good be-haviour—*the man who does right...is righteous*. Claims to a right standing with God, separated from right behaviour, are meaningless. This leads on to the thought (verse 8) that *the man who sins* reveals himself as *a child of the devil*. This does not mean, of course, that the devil has anything to do with the origin or creation of a sinful man; it is simply that sinful be-haviour reveals a kind of family likeness, to be seen in all those whose behaviour is of the sort favoured by 'the devil'. Then the writer comes round once more to the thought (verse 8, end) that the purpose of the appearance of the Son of God was to undo *the devil's work*.

Our writer has no difficulty in thinking of *the devil* as a kind of permanent enemy of God and all his purposes. In itself this tells us nothing as to whether 'there is' a devil. It does show us that in these early days of the Church the leaders of the Church felt themselves confronted with a powerful force of evil, and personal language was that which came naturally to their tongues and pens when they spoke or wrote of it. The idea of Christ's battle with the devil, or devils, is clearly present in Matt. 12: 28, 'it is by the Spirit of God that I drive out the devils'.

The third paragraph (verses 9–12) develops the idea from the standpoint of what characterizes 'a child of God' (verse 9). The author has been led into this train of thought by using the phrase, in the previous paragraph 'a child of the devil'. It is as though he said, 'Being a child of the devil is shown by living a life of sin—what are the signs of being a child of God?' The chief sign, he goes on, is that the person con-cerned *does not commit sin* (verse 9). He does not do this, we are told, *because the divine seed remains in him*. Probably what he meant by this was something like what we mean when we say of someone, 'He's exactly like his father', or, 'Of course, he's got it in him: his father was a great musician'—or golfer, or what you will. He may have had prominently in his mind the picture of physical generation as in the botanical or animal world by the fertilization of the female *ovum* or egg with the male *semen* or seed. This figure was used by Jewish and Christian writers of the period. Of the Hebrew nation Philo says (*Life of Moses*, I, 279), 'Their bodies were moulded of human seeds, but their souls of divine; wherefore they have become kinsfolk of God'. It may well be that in seeking to rebut wild ideas of certain gnostics (e.g. that behaviour did not matter so long as you had the key of knowledge), the writer has borrowed this idea of the implanted seed with which to make his point. The idea of Christians deriving their birth from some spiritual 'seed' is seen in John 1: 12, 13, 'children of God, not born of any human stock, or by the fleshly desire of a human father, but the offspring of God himself'. Also in 1 Pet. 1: 23–5, 'born anew, not of mortal parentage but of immortal, through the living and enduring word of God' and in James 1: 18, 'by declaring the truth, he gave us birth'.

Notice how verse 10 says *no one who does not do right is God's child*, and then it adds *nor is anyone who does not love his brother*. It is as though he were saying 'it is not enough to live a decent, law-abiding life—there must be seen also "that most excellent gift of charity", that unselfish love which is the special characteristic of Christ's followers when being inspired by their master'.

Love one another (verse 11) is the true, authentic, original Christian command. The writer illustrates what he means by a case of the extreme *opposite* attitude—that of Cain (Gen. 4: 1–15). His murderous and jealous nature marked him out (verse 12) as *a child of the evil one*.

It is rather difficult to accept, in modern times, this clear-cut, black-and-white distinction between *children of God* and *children of the devil*, between sinners and non-sinners. Even this letter is not always consistent. In 1: 8 it said, 'If we claim to be sinless, we are self-deceived'. Now it says (verse 9), *a child of God does not commit sin*. Many efforts have been made to harmonize these apparently contradictory statements. • One line of argument is to slip in the word 'habitually' or 'continually' in verse 9—reading then 'a child of God does not commit sin habitually, i.e. as a regular practice'. There is some support for this in the Greek original but the distinction is a subtle one, and not very obvious. It is more natural to accept the view that both statements are argumentative, polemical. Against those who boast a sinless record, the writer says, 'this is self-deception'. As Paul says, 'all alike have sinned'—our writer would agree with that. But against those who say 'Sin doesn't matter' he says 'God's children do not sin'. Both statements are true in their context, but neither contains the whole truth; they are complementary the one to the other. ✳

LIFE MEANS LOVE

My brothers, do not be surprised if the world hates you. 13
We for our part have crossed over from death to life; this 14
we know, because we love our brothers. The man who
does not love is still in the realm of death, for everyone 15
who hates his brother is a murderer, and no murderer, as
you know, has eternal life within him. It is by this that 16
we know what love is: that Christ laid down his life for us.
And we in our turn are bound to lay down our lives for
our brothers. But if a man has enough to live on, and 17
yet when he sees his brother in need shuts up his heart
against him, how can it be said that the divine love dwells
in him?

✳ This paragraph weaves a complicated pattern of thought with a number of contrasting opposites: life–death; love–hate; murdering–laying down one's life for others. The readers are first warned not to be surprised if they are confronted with the hatred of the world. They have already been warned (1: 15–17) not to love 'the world'; now they must steel themselves to accept the world's hate. Exactly the same thought is to be found in the Gospel (John 15: 17–19, 'If the world hates you, it hated me first, as you know well. If you belonged to the world, the world would love its own; but because you do not belong to the world, because I have chosen you out of the world, for that reason the world hates you'). Our writer has this sense of a clear frontier between those who make up the family of God's reborn children (i.e. the Christians or the Church) and those who make up the rest of humanity, which he calls 'the world'.

The readers are not to be in doubt or anxiety about their own position. '"We" [i.e. writer and readers] know that we have crossed the frontier from death to life—this knowledge springs from the fact that we are bound up with our fellow-Christians in love and mutual concern.' It is noticeable that while the Synoptic Gospels speak mainly of our duty to our *neighbours*, the Johannine literature speaks of love for 'the brother' or 'brothers'. It is difficult to avoid the conclusion that by the end of the first century the Christian community had become clearly defined, and that it was in this sphere that mutual obligation was most fully realized.

To be without love is to be *in the realm of death*—for no love means hatred, and hating is murder, and to be a murderer is incompatible with being filled with eternal life, which is love. All this sounds very extreme, indeed far-fetched. But in Matt. 5: 21, 22 Jesus says that to nurse anger is to court judgement, just as murder was known to do. Here the point is made still more strongly. The progress from the absence of love to the status of 'murderer' is very rapid. Our writer saw all in black and white; for him there was no grey.

Turning rapidly to the opposite side of the coin (verse 16) he says that there is one way by which we know what love is, what it consists of. This is by contemplating the supreme example of love, the fact of Christ laying down his life for men. Far from hating men, far from seeking to destroy them,

40

he voluntarily laid down his *own* life for them. Loving sacrifice is contrasted with hating destructiveness.

Belief that the death of Jesus was in some sense a voluntary act done out of love for men is deeply rooted in the New Testament (see, e.g. Gal. 2: 20, 'the Son of God, who loved me and sacrificed himself for me'; see also Rom. 5: 8).

Here is an example on which Christian character is to be based. The 'imitation of Christ' is a constant theme in the New Testament (see, e.g. 2 Cor. 8: 9, 'For you know how generous our Lord Jesus Christ has been'; see also 2 Cor. 10: 1; Phil. 2: 2–8). We are told here that we are *to lay down our lives for our brothers*. That sounds frightening, but it is at least challenging. A sudden example of what may be needed (verse 17) brings the readers down to earth with a bump. If you have enough to live on, and can peacefully see your brother *in need*, the divine love cannot be in you. Modern readers are surely justified in treating the word *brother* in the widest sense. All men are our brothers in the human family, and nowadays all are neighbours. A famine relief project is as much a Christian concern as a coin for a beggar at the door. ✳

LOVE MUST BE PRACTICAL

My children, love must not be a matter of words or talk; 18 it must be genuine, and show itself in action. This is how 19 we may know that we belong to the realm of truth, and convince ourselves in his sight that even if our conscience 20 condemns us, God is greater than our conscience and knows all.

✳ This little paragraph is mostly recapitulation—love is not a matter of high-sounding words or phrases, it is a matter of practical behaviour (*action*) and genuine reality (verse 18). This practical self-giving life will prove to be a source of confidence and assurance. We can tell from it that we are in *the realm of* *truth* (a variant for 'life'). This practical proof of being 'right with God' will sustain our confidence *in his sight*, even though our conscience is aware of many failings. Objective goodness is put above subjective self-depreciation. The second alternative translation in the N.E.B. margin gives the idea that 'if even our own conscience condemns us, still more will God, who is greater than conscience'. *

CONFIDENT FELLOWSHIP WITH GOD

21 Dear friends, if our conscience does not condemn us, then
22 we can approach God with confidence, and obtain from him whatever we ask, because we are keeping his com-
23 mands and doing what he approves. This is his command: to give our allegiance to his Son Jesus Christ and love one
24 another as he commanded. When we keep his commands we dwell in him and he dwells in us. And this is how we can make sure that he dwells within us: we know it from the Spirit he has given us.

* The first sentence picks up the last of the previous paragraphs. *Conscience* may condemn, but it is still possible to trust in God's greatness and omniscience. Once this step is taken the conscience does *not* condemn, and that is where this paragraph begins (verse 21). If we are in this happy state we have *confidence* (*parrhēsia*, a Greek word suggesting freedom of speech and conversation) with God. We *obtain from him whatever we ask*—this is an overstatement, for no Christian could truthfully make such a sweeping claim. It does suggest, however, a life in which there is a trustful interchange between the child of God and his Father, in which prayer is a reality, and 'answers to prayer' common. This trust goes with obedience— *keeping his commands and doing what he approves* (verse 22).

This leads on to a summing up of what God's commandment is: *to give our allegiance to his Son Jesus Christ and love one*

another (verse 23). *Give our allegiance* is the N.E.B. translation
of the familiar word *believe*, put trust in (Greek *pisteuō*). The
original Greek stresses the act of putting trust in, confiding in.
Doubtless this is what the translators were trying to convey.
This *faith* is put alongside *love* (verse 23), reminding us of the
frequent bringing together of these two great ideas in the
writings of Paul (e.g. Eph. 3: 17). Moral obedience is the
only secret of spiritual union—the one who keeps God's
commands dwells in God and God dwells in him (verse 24).
Finally, one more way is chosen to express the basis of this
confident life of fellowship with God: *this is how we can make
sure that he dwells within us: we know it from the Spirit he has
given us* (verse 24, end). *Spirit* is given a capital letter by our
translators, probably rightly, in view of 1 John 4: 13, where
almost the same sentence occurs—but there we read 'he has
imparted his Spirit to us' (literally, 'he has given us from his
Spirit'). The author does not mean *spirit* in the sense of having
a certain *spirit* or *character*: though the sign of the presence of
the Holy Spirit is to be seen in the character and deeds which
reflect the character of the self-giving Christ. ✳

TEST THE SPIRITS!

But do not trust any and every spirit, my friends; test the 4
spirits, to see whether they are from God, for among
those who have gone out into the world there are many
prophets falsely inspired. This is how we may recognize 2
the Spirit of God: every spirit which acknowledges that
Jesus Christ has come in the flesh is from God, and every 3
spirit which does not thus acknowledge Jesus is not from
God. This is what is meant by 'Antichrist'; you have
been told that he was to come, and here he is, in the world
already!

But you, my children, are of God's family, and you 4

have the mastery over these false prophets, because he
who inspires you is greater than he who inspires the god-
5 less world. They are of that world, and so therefore is their
6 teaching; that is why the world listens to them. But we
belong to God, and a man who knows God listens to us,
while he who does not belong to God refuses us a hearing.
That is how we distinguish the spirit of truth from the
spirit of error.

✵ These two paragraphs contain some of the most significant
and characteristic teaching of the letter, part of it being closely
paralleled in the second letter.

In order to enter into it, we must visualize the atmosphere
of the primitive church. We must rid ourselves of the material-
istic, scientific atmosphere of the twentieth century, and picture a time when the earth was full of strange spirits, at least
that is how it seemed to the minds of those then living. When
people broke out into wild, ecstatic speech or song, this was
at once put down to some form of spirit-possession. Religious
excitement has often led to extraordinary physical phenomena,
e.g. in the time of John Wesley (eighteenth century) it was
common for those who heard him to fall to the ground and
to cry and moan under the influence of his preaching. In the
first century this would have been put down to spirit-possession, a possession that might be thought of as the work of the
Holy Spirit, bringing first conviction of sin and then the peace
of forgiveness, or alternatively as the work of evil spirits, having
as it were a 'last fling' before handing over their prey to the
Lordship of Christ. Examples of the latter can be seen in Mark
9: 25–7 and Acts 16: 16–18.

When men and women in the Church were carried away
in this manner they were said to be 'prophesying'. If they
were regularly found to have this gift, they were 'prophets'.
The stress was not on any power to foretell the future, though
this was sometimes included (see Acts 11: 27–30). To keep

such 'prophesyings' under control was something of a problem in the early Church, as we see from I Cor. 12 and 14. In
these chapters Paul distinguishes between 'prophecy', by
which he seems to mean preaching under the influence of the
spirit of God, and 'ecstatic utterance', by which he means
speaking unintelligible words or sounds under the same influence. There was a place for the latter (I Cor. 14: 39) but it
was better when it was interpreted into ordinary speech. Even
'prophecy' needed some discipline in its exercise (I Cor. 14: 29
—only two or three speakers were needed). There was a danger
that people might be thought to be speaking under God's influence when in fact they were controlled by evil spirits. Paul
gives a crude example in I Cor. 12: 3: 'I must impress upon you
that no one who says "A curse on Jesus!" can be speaking
under the influence of the Spirit of God. And no one can say
"Jesus is Lord!", except under the influence of the Holy Spirit.'
In other words, the test of the 'holiness' of the spirit animating
such an utterance was how far the utterance exalted Jesus as
the source of all truth and the seat of all authority. It is the
very same point that arises in the first letter of John.

There were apparently some who were ready to *trust any
and every spirit* (verse 1). This was a mistake. They had to *test
the spirits*, to discover whether or not they were from God.
The N.E.B. says *among those who have gone out into the world
there are many prophets falsely inspired.* As the translators were
working from the usual modern text they seem to have made
the meaning more involved than it is. The original Greek
simply says 'many false prophets have gone out into the world'.
The really interesting point is the meaning of 'gone out'—out
from where? In I John 2: 19 we read, in connexion with the
many antichrists, 'They went out from our company, but
never really belonged to us', the 'went out' of the original
being interpreted as going out or away from the Church into
a life of heretical teaching. But in 2 John 7, 8, in a passage almost
identical with the one now being considered, we read 'many
deceivers have gone out into the world, who do not acknow-

ledge Jesus Christ as coming in the flesh. These are the persons described as the Antichrist, the arch-deceiver. Beware of them....' Thus although the 'going out' *could* be the going out from the Church into the world, it is slightly more probable that the writer means 'many false prophets have appeared, come out—possibly from the sphere of darkness—and are now abroad, spreading error and causing danger to those who hear them'.

If it comes to a test, this is provided in verse 2: *every spirit which acknowledges that Jesus Christ has come in the flesh is from God, and every spirit which does not thus acknowledge Jesus is not from God.* We are at once reminded of Paul's similar test (p. 45). Here, however, the test is not just whether or not 'Jesus is Lord', it is related to the manner of his Incarnation. The docetists (see pp. 9, 10) could not accept the fact that Jesus had been a real man in every sense of the word, had really 'come in the flesh'. Hence our writer's stress on this particular aspect of the faith which he considered necessary. As elsewhere (I John 2: 18, 22) he relates this false teaching to the idea of Antichrist. They were prepared for some kind of terrible 'antichristian' outburst—this he said was it: *here he is, in the world already* (verse 3).

Now he turns, as elsewhere, to give his readers confidence and hope. *But you, my children, are of God's family* (verse 4)— the Greek says 'you are *of God*', but the paraphrase in the N.E.B. is legitimate—'of God' may mean 'sprung from God', as in 3: 9. They have already mastered these false prophets, because the one who indwells and inspires them is greater than the spirit which dominates the world outside (the N.E.B. says '*godless* world', again paraphrasing to make the meaning clear). Their teaching (i.e. that of the false prophets) is inspired by the same spirit as is the world in general (*they are of that world*, verse 5). So it is that they get a good hearing— *that is why the world listens to them. We*, he says, meaning writer and readers together, *belong to God*, and those who know God listen to them (verse 6). It is difficult to see exactly what he

means by *a man who knows God*. In John 17: 3 to know God is
treated as the equivalent of eternal life: 'This is eternal life: to
know thee who alone art truly God, and Jesus Christ whom
thou hast sent.' But here he may refer to those in the Church
who are truly in tune with God's mind and will, and hence
ready to welcome and keep the teaching which he believes to
come from God. He may alternatively refer to an inward
disposition in those who hear the gospel, something in them
disposing them to hear and obey. If so, we find the same idea
(that some are *predestined* to believe) in the Gospel (see, e.g.
John 17: 6, 'I have made thy name known to the men whom
thou didst give me out of the world. They were thine, thou
gavest them to me, and they have obeyed thy command').
Our writer saw things in black and white: for him there was
no grey. If it is difficult to speak in quite such clear-cut terms
today it is still true that some people seem 'to have it in them'
to respond to the Church's message and to adhere to it; others
seem to lack the wavelength on which they can receive the
message. ✳

GOD THE SOURCE OF LOVE—AND ITS STANDARD

Dear friends, let us love one another, because love is from 7
God. Everyone who loves is a child of God and knows
God, but the unloving know nothing of God. For God 8
is love; and his love was disclosed to us in this, that he 9
sent his only Son into the world to bring us life. The love 10
I speak of is not our love for God, but the love he showed
to us in sending his Son as the remedy for the defilement
of our sins. If God thus loved us, dear friends, we in turn 11
are bound to love one another. Though God has never 12
been seen by any man, God himself dwells in us if
we love one another; his love is brought to perfection
within us.

✳ This paragraph picks up the thread of the argument where it was dropped at 3 : 24. The writer was dealing with the necessity of mutual love (3 : 23) and was led on to refer to 'the Spirit he has given us'. This in turn led to the digression on testing the spirits (4: 1–6). Now he returns to the main thread. Mutual love (verse 7) is of infinite importance because *love is from God.* When he says that *everyone who loves is a child of God and knows God* he certainly does not mean that in every person who feels some surge of emotional love—man for woman, mother for child—there is the sign of this God-given love, indicating God-given life. There may be some links between the most elementary forms of love—even that of a mother-bird for its young—and the divine love, but that is not what our writer is thinking about. *God is love* (verse 8), he states, and he will repeat it at verse 16. By this he means that God's whole nature and being is best summed up by the word 'love'; he does not mean that 'love is God'. This is made clear by the historic evidence he at once brings forward: *his love was disclosed to us in this, that he sent his only Son into the world to bring us life.* (The N.E.B. has paraphrased the last group of words: the Greek has 'so that we should live through him'.) These words echo very closely, though not precisely, the famous summary of the Gospel in John 3 : 16, 'God loved the world so much that he gave his only Son, that everyone who has faith in him may not die but have eternal life'. In both texts the Incarnation is said to be a demonstration of God's love. In both Jesus is described as 'only Son'. In both the purpose of the Incarnation is felt to be the giving of life to the world, or at least to believers. To make his point abundantly clear, he says plainly that the love he is speaking of as coming 'from God' is not our love, not even our love for God, but God's love for us. This found its supreme expression in the coming of Jesus, but still more precisely in the purpose of that coming— he was to be *the remedy for the defilement of our sins* (verse 10). For the phrase 'remedy for the defilement' (Greek *hilasmos*) see notes on 2: 2. Because all Christians owe everything to

this torrent of love, poured into the world and into the hearts
of Christians, mutual love becomes a privilege and an obligation. For *God has never been seen by any man* (verse 12) but
through the mutual love of Christians God's love comes to its
full fruit; it *is brought to perfection* (verse 12). ✳

LOVE DEPENDS ON FAITH

Here is the proof that we dwell in him and he dwells in 13
us: he has imparted his Spirit to us. Moreover, we have 14
seen for ourselves, and we attest, that the Father sent the
Son to be the saviour of the world, and if a man acknow- 15
ledges that Jesus is the Son of God, God dwells in him and
he dwells in God. Thus we have come to know and believe 16
the love which God has for us.

✳ Our writer means to go round and round this theme of
God's 'indwelling' of Christians and their 'dwelling in God'
and here he reminds them that right belief is important as
well as right emotion or behaviour. The great assurance that
Christians have, he says, is the presence of the Holy Spirit in
their hearts and in their fellowship. (He has already made this
point in 3: 24; he returns to it in 4: 13.) In both 3: 24 and in
4: 13 the Greek has, rather pointedly, 'he has given us "from",
or "out of", his spirit'. The N.E.B. has not thought it necessary to stress this point, which is in any case awkward to
express in English. There is, however, an important suggestion
that no individual 'has' the whole Holy Spirit: he has his or her
share in the Spirit which fills the whole Church. But to the
inward testimony of the Spirit (an indefinable experience
which is always the most first-hand authority to which any
one can appeal) there is added the common, corporate grip on
the historic fact that *the Father sent the Son to be the saviour of
the world* (verse 14). Another way of putting this was to say
(verse 15) *Jesus is the Son of God*. In these first days of the

Church, to say that Jesus was the Son of God was not so much to make a 'supernatural' (*metaphysical*) statement about his nature, as to say that his whole life was an act of God, so intimately expressing the Father's mind and will that the one who carried it through could only be called his Son, indeed his only Son. Hence this life of faith, this act of witness was another doorway through which the Christian could enter upon the life of union with God that the writer describes so often as one of mutual 'indwelling'. It is a doorway, because it leads to knowledge of and faith in God's love for us; hence, by implication, it leads to a life of love, and hence to a life of fellowship with God. ✳

LOVE BRINGS CONFIDENCE, BUT IT MUST BE REAL LOVE

God is love; he who dwells in love is dwelling in God,
17 and God in him. This is for us the perfection of love, to have confidence on the day of judgement, and this we
18 can have, because even in this world we are as he is. There is no room for fear in love; perfect love banishes fear. For fear brings with it the pains of judgement, and anyone
19 who is afraid has not attained to love in its perfection. We
20 love because he loved us first. But if a man says, 'I love God', while hating his brother, he is a liar. If he does not love the brother whom he has seen, it cannot be that he
21 loves God whom he has not seen. And indeed this command comes to us from Christ himself: that he who loves God must also love his brother.

✳ The writer opens another paragraph with the thought that has dominated the last two paragraphs—*God is love; he who dwells in love is dwelling in God, and God in him.* This is virtually a repetition of 4: 12. But now he develops it in a new way.

He sees in this relationship a source of confidence which even the coming of *the day of judgement* cannot destroy. His thought is very closely packed just here, but what he seems to mean is this: God's love, having flowed *to* us through Christ, reaches its climax when it flows *through* us to others—*This is for us the perfection of love* (verse 17). But when this is so, there is a real similarity between our situation *even in this world* and the situation Christ was in when God's love flowed through him. Such an identity of situation (however imperfectly achieved) makes fear for the future impossible—*perfect love banishes fear*. The thought is very much like that of Paul in Rom. 8: 35-9, 'what can separate us from the love of Christ?...there is... nothing in all creation that can separate us from the love of God in Christ Jesus our Lord'. Fear, we read, *brings with it the pains of judgement* (verse 18). It anticipates, and makes real the pains it fears and contemplates. The writer correctly sees that such an attitude indicates a faulty love-relationship with God (verse 18).

In verse 19 we find one of those striking short sentences containing a wealth of meaning: *We love because he loved us first*. Some familiar versions of the Bible used to read *We love him* or *we love God*, but the N.E.B. has followed the more generally approved text which says just *we love*. This is really a more far-reaching assertion than *we love God*. It means that because of God's act of love in Jesus Christ something has come into our hearts which releases a stream of love flowing out both to God and man. Paul says, in Rom. 5: 5, 'God's love has flooded our inmost heart through the Holy Spirit he has given us'.

The last verses of the chapter are devoted to a practical test of true love for God. *If a man says, 'I love God', while hating his brother, he is a liar*. The writer holds that it is impossible to love the unseen God, and to hate the brother who is visible. This argument has not always been found convincing. Some have said, 'I perhaps could love my brother if I had not seen him, but having seen and known him, I cannot!' But our writer sees things differently. He says: 'Love to God, as a mystical emotion, is meaningless. The way to prove the reality of this love is by loving God's other children, i.e. your brothers.' He rapidly backs this up by claiming the authority of 'Christ himself', i.e. the historic Jesus, for this very same principle. He is probably thinking of Mark 12: 30, 31: 'love the Lord your God with all your heart....Love your neighbour as yourself'.

It is worth noting that Jesus says 'neighbour'—any one who proves to be 'nigh' or 'near' to you. Our writer says *brother* and apparently he always means by this 'fellow-Christian'. It is a feature of the Johannine literature that the circle of believers is regarded as the sphere in which Christian love is to be exercised. We have moved far from the words of Jesus 'Love your enemies' (Matt. 5: 45). We have even left behind 'Love your neighbour'. Probably by the time these Johannine books were written the Church had become a self-contained, often hard-hit, persecuted community, and it seemed to provide a sufficient sphere in which to exercise Christian love. In the Fourth Gospel (John 15: 13) we read, 'There is no greater love than this, that a man should lay down his life *for his friends*'. Even the love of Jesus himself, in that Gospel is peculiarly directed to his own friends (e.g. John 13: 1, 'He had always loved *his own* who were in the world, and now he was to show the full extent of his love').

Augustine, preaching about this book at Hippo in North Africa in A.D. 415, was much concerned over this point. He fell back on an ingenious, if far-fetched way of reconciling the two commands 'love your enemies' and 'love your brother'. His idea was this. If you love an enemy you do not love him *as* an enemy, but in order to win him from his enmity, to friendship. So in loving your enemy you are really loving your friend, though that friend has not yet been brought into existence. So, he goes on, loving your brother includes loving your enemy. He was using his subtle logical mind to solve a problem. He hardly solved it, but at least he shows us that he understood the problem clearly enough.

In the last resort the close coherence of the Christian fellow-ship may be a means whereby it gives itself for, and gives its witness to, the whole of humanity. ✲

CHRISTIAN FAITH—SOURCE OF LOVE AND VICTORY

Everyone who believes that Jesus is the Christ is a child of **5** God, and to love the parent means to love his child; it ₂ follows that when we love God and obey his commands we love his children too. For to love God is to keep his ₃ commands; and they are not burdensome, because every ₄ child of God is victor over the godless world. The victory that defeats the world is our faith, for who is victor over ₅ the world but he who believes that Jesus is the Son of God?

✲ The opening words of this chapter, in the form given in the N.E.B., follow fairly naturally from the end of chapter 4. In this form they are meant to give a convincing reason for love within the Christian fellowship. The argument is this. The man who *believes that Jesus is the Christ is a child of God* (verse 1). This echoes 4: 15, and Paul's words in Gal. 3: 26, 'Through faith you are all sons of God in union with Christ Jesus'. If you love God (the claim made in 4: 20, 'I love God') you must love all his children, i.e. your fellow-believers. This is what is meant when it says *to love the parent means to love his child* (5: 1). *It follows that* if we are really loving God in a practical way—keeping his commandments—we love God's children too (5: 2).

The N.E.B. translation has some good grounding. It at least makes a logical sequence of some rather queerly linked sentences. But it is not entirely beyond question. It has these difficulties. In 3: 13 the love of fellow-Christians—something tangible—is given as a proof of having crossed the frontier from death to life. One would have expected this same love to be a proof of true love to God, but the N.E.B. makes the opposite sense. The N.E.B. says 'loving God implies loving God's children'. Then the N.E.B. skips rather lightly over the Greek of 5: 2. The literal translation is, 'In this we know that we love the children of God whenever we love God', etc. 'It follows that' is a very free rendering of 'in this we know'. But even if that verse were differently handled the difficulty mentioned above would remain. Could it be that the writer, or a very early copyist, himself made a mistake? It would have been so much easier if we had found this in our letter: 'By this we know that we love God and keep his commandments, when we love the children of God.' Still there is no evidence that he *did* write that. All we can say is that if he had it would have been in line with what he says elsewhere.

Now he is led on along another path. *Can* we keep God's commandments? Yes, he says, we can. Every child of God is a victor over his hostile environment (verse 4). The key to victory is faith, faith in Jesus as the Son of God. Such faith unites the believer to the Son of God, who himself 'conquered' *his* hostile environment, and cried from the cross, 'It is accomplished' (John 19: 30). While the Johannine literature says much about 'believing' it rarely mentions the noun *faith*—this is one example of its use. In Paul 'faith' is a most frequent word. ✳

DIVINE TESTIMONY TO JESUS AS SON OF GOD

6 This is he who came with water and blood: Jesus Christ. He came, not by water alone, but by water and blood;
7 and there is the Spirit to bear witness, because the Spirit is
8 truth. For there are three witnesses, the Spirit, the water,
9 and the blood, and these three are in agreement. We accept human testimony, but surely divine testimony is stronger, and this threefold testimony is indeed that of God himself,
10 the witness he has borne to his Son. He who believes in

the Son of God has this testimony in his own heart, but he who disbelieves God, makes him out to be a liar, by refusing to accept God's own witness to his Son. The 11 witness is this: that God has given us eternal life, and that this life is found in his Son. He who possesses the Son has 12 life indeed; he who does not possess the Son of God has not that life.

✻ This is an important paragraph intended to summarize and clinch the argument of the letter, and in particular to emphasize that God's own authority has been stamped upon the truth of the Christian gospel. Verses 6–8 must be read as a whole and the statements in them noted and listed. These statements are, briefly summarized: (*a*) Jesus Christ came both 'by' water and 'by' blood, (*b*) the Spirit, which is truth, bears witness of this, (*c*) Spirit, water and blood all unite to give one message, one testimony.

Before attempting to clarify these mysterious words, it is necessary to read some words in the Gospel (John 19: 34, 35): 'One of the soldiers stabbed his side with a lance, and at once there was a flow of blood and water. This is vouched for by an eyewitness, whose evidence is to be trusted. He knows that he speaks the truth, so that you too may believe.' It seems certain that there is *some* connexion between these two passages. Unfortunately we do not know for certain which was written first, but it is usual to think that the Gospel (its main part at least) was written before the letters. If so, our writer knew, and probably himself penned, the words in John 19: 34, 35. This passage (alone among the four accounts of the crucifixion) recorded this incident immediately after the death of Jesus—the piercing of the side, and the outpouring of blood and water. Great emphasis is placed on the reliability of the witness given. The 'truth' is assured, that faith may follow: 'He knows that he speaks the truth, so that you too may believe.'

If we explain the words in the Gospel by other passages in

the same Gospel (and that is the safest procedure) we note these points: (*a*) To enter the kingdom of God, you must be born 'from water and spirit' (John 3: 5); (*b*) to eat Christ's flesh and to drink his blood is to have eternal life (John 6: 54); (*c*) the Spirit which Christians 'would receive later' is pictured under the figure of 'streams of living water' flowing from Christ (John 7: 38, 39). Thus in the experience by which Christians came to their new life and were maintained in it there were elements described as water, blood, flesh, spirit (and the close connexion between 'spirit' and 'air' must not be forgotten). Water is linked with spirit, and in one place identified with it. Blood was bracketed with flesh. In the light of all this, what the Evangelist *probably* meant in 19: 34, 35 was this. 'After Jesus died blood and water flowed from his pierced, but un-broken body. This shows that his very life—his blood, which is the life, and his spirit, pictured by the water—is flowing out into the world in cleansing, revivifying, refreshing power.' Probably he felt that the water of baptism and the wine of the Lord's Supper permanently symbolized, perhaps more than symbolized, these divine graces.

Against all this 'allegorical' interpretation, it may be thought that all the Evangelist wants to say is this: Jesus *really* died; he did not *seem* to die. Someone saw the blood and water flowing from his wounded side. Therefore he *really* died.

Now after this long digression we come back to 1 John 5: 6–8. Here we have 'water *and blood*', not 'blood and water'—the stress is on the presence of the 'blood'. This suggests that there were some (as we know there were) who said Jesus Christ came only 'by water' (i.e. the Son of God descended on Jesus at this baptism, and left him before his blood was shed). Now this truth does not depend on the presence of a human eyewitness (cf. John 19: 35) but on the evidence of the Spirit—an invisible witness, but one whose evidence is irrefutable: he *is* truth (verse 6).

Now the writer puts these three ideas together and calls them all witnesses—spirit, water, and blood. Their witness is not contradictory, it is harmonious. Who can say *exactly* what he meant by this cryptic utterance? Probably no one, with complete accuracy; but if you imagine he meant something like this you may not be far wrong: Jesus came into the world; his ministry took place between two great moments, his baptism and his death. The spirit descended on him at his baptism and after his death he breathed that spirit into his disciples. In the hearts of Christian people, and especially in their fellowship and worship, that Spirit speaks with irresistible authority. In the waters of baptism, in the wine of communion the Spirit speaks and acts, giving new life, cleansing from sin, bestowing on the Jesus of history a living, contemporary authority which those who know it recognize to be nothing less than 'divine testimony' (verse 9).

[The Authorized Version has after verse 6 these words: 'For there are three that bear record in heaven, the Father, the Word, and the Holy Ghost: and these three are one. And there are three that bear witness on earth, the spirit, and the water, and the blood: and these three agree in one.' It is known that the extra words crept into the text in the fourth century, coming first into the Latin version. Those who valued the clear teaching of the Church about the Trinity (Three Persons and one God) could not resist the temptation to put three 'Heavenly Witnesses' alongside the three witnesses of the letter, who are then called witnesses as *on earth*. The incident is interesting from the point of view of textual history, and of doctrinal history, but it is really irrelevant to a study of I John as it was first written. Possibly the added passage was suggested by verse 9 'this threefold testimony is indeed that of God himself'.]

In verse 10 the writer gives a grand statement of what is called the 'internal testimony of the Holy Spirit', *He who believes in the Son of God has this testimony in his own heart*. The second half of his sentence, in which he says that disbelievers 'make God out to be a liar' is not so convincing. Verses 11 and 12 sum up the whole letter—God has given eternal life; this life is in his Son. To *possess* the Son is to possess life; not to possess him is not to possess life.

Although there are nine verses still to come, verse 12 is the real *finale* of the letter—true life is to be found only in 'the Son', i.e. in faith in and fellowship with Jesus Christ, who, as Son, opens the way to fellowship with the Father. Verses like 6–8, with their mysterious reference to 'blood' and 'water' may seem to move in a world far removed from our own. But in the end the message is expressed in simpler, more timeless language. It is as true today as ever it was (so Christians believe) that 'life indeed', true life, eternal life, is to be found from one source alone, from Jesus, God's Word to men. That Word is to be heard, in part, in all that is true, beautiful and good—even where the name of Jesus is unknown, or rejected. But it is heard fully, clearly, decisively in Jesus Christ, in the historic Jesus, his words and deeds, and in the living Christ, active in and through his Church in all the world. ✳

ASSURED CONFIDENCE—ESPECIALLY IN PRAYER

13 This letter is to assure you that you have eternal life. It is addressed to those who give their allegiance to the Son of God.

14 We can approach God with confidence for this reason: if we make requests which accord with his will he listens
15 to us; and if we know that our requests are heard, we know also that the things we ask for are ours.

16 If a man sees his brother committing a sin which is not a deadly sin, he should pray to God for him, and he will grant him life—that is, when men are not guilty of deadly sin. There is such a thing as deadly sin, and I do not
17 suggest that he should pray about that; but although all wrongdoing is sin, not all sin is deadly sin.

* The first sentence of this section gives a reason for writing and sending the letter—it might have been intended as the concluding sentence of the letter. Its similarity to the last verse of the Fourth Gospel in what we think was its original form (John 20: 31) is most striking. Almost every word in our verse has its parallel in the other. It is one of the clearest indications of a common authorship.

Notice the close parallels—which are shown here in a literal translation from the Greek:

> Letter: These things I have written to you so that
> Gospel: These things are written so that

> Letter: you may know that you have eternal life
> Gospel: you may believe that Jesus is the Christ

> Letter: you who believe in the name of the Son of God
> Gospel: the Son of God, and so that believing you may have
> life in his name.

Those who pray from within this Christian revelation can do so *with confidence* (verse 14). Our requests must be those *which accord with his will*, then we can be sure that *he listens*—more than this, we can feel that *the things we ask for are ours* (verse 15). Many phrases are used in the New Testament to show that Christian prayers have to be brought into line with God's purpose, e.g. John 14: 13, 'anything you ask *in my name* I will do'. How to harmonize the firm promises of Scripture about prayer with the very mixed results of the 'answers to prayer' which we receive has always been and probably always will be a problem to Christian people. On the one hand there is a firm conviction that prayer is not useless, not meaningless. Often, surprising things happen that we are sure are connected with prayers, our own or others. But often nothing extraordinary, or nothing extraordinarily good appears to happen. Conventional teachers sometimes explain this by saying that the prayer was not 'according to God's will', or not offered in sufficient faith. Such explanations are inadequate. We can only take the broad teaching of the New Testament, and accept the fact that the partial experiences of men cannot be brought into a fully coherent system. We are taught to pray; we are taught to pray 'according to God's will'; we are taught to pray in faith. But we have the example of the prayer of Jesus in Gethsemane (Mark 14: 36) to remind us that it is not possible for all the best prayers of even the best people to be answered as they would wish.

One particular form of prayer is commended (verses 16 and 17). It is prayer for a *brother* who is seen to be *committing a sin*. Prayer for such a man *will* be answered says our writer, and God will give him life. But there is a sin, he says, where this may not apply—the 'deadly sin', the sin *pros thanaton*, leading to death. What was this sin? We cannot say. All we know is that at different points in the New Testament (e.g. Mark 3: 28, 29) there is reference to sin of a kind which cannot be forgiven. In Mark this sin is 'slandering the Holy Spirit'. In Heb. 6: 5, 6 it is falling away after experiencing the full blessings of Christianity. Probably our writer meant by *deadly sin* a permanent and deliberate rejection of the true faith in favour of the old paganism or some new heresy. He does not *forbid* prayer for the victim of such a temptation, but he does not feel that he can confidently order such prayer (verse 16— *I do not suggest that he should pray about that.* The translation is rather stronger than the original Greek because 'I do not suggest' is stronger than the Greek 'I do not *say*'). *

THREE THINGS THAT WE KNOW

18 We know that no child of God is a sinner; it is the Son of God who keeps him safe, and the evil one cannot touch him.

19 We know that we are of God's family, while the whole godless world lies in the power of the evil one.

20 We know that the Son of God has come and given us

understanding to know him who is real; indeed we are in him who is real, since we are in his Son Jesus Christ. This is the true God, this is eternal life. My children, be on the 21 watch against false gods.

* The letter closes with three great assertions, each introduced by *we know*.

The first picks up the thought of 3: 9 and stresses that *no child of God is a sinner*. Lawless behaviour in a Christian is ruled out, through the protection of the Son of God, who keeps him out of the clutches of *the evil one* (verse 18). This verse supports the view that 'Deliver us from evil' in the Lord's Prayer originally meant 'Save us from the evil one', as in the N.E.B. at Matt. 6: 13.

The second assertion is of the sharp division between the Church and the world. The Church is 'of God' (translated rather freely in the N.E.B. as *of God's family*). The point is almost certainly that Christians are divided off from the god-less world which is in the grip of the evil one, but it *could* be an assertion that '*we*', i.e. the writer and his associates were 'of God' rather than their heretical opponents.

The third assertion is a statement of the main point of the Christian creed, *the Son of God has come* (verse 20). This coming has produced an understanding of the real one, the true one, i.e. God. Christians are *in* God because they are in, i.e. linked to and surrounded by Jesus Christ. *This is the true God, this is eternal life.* These words are almost identical with the words of Jesus in John 17: 3: 'This is eternal life: to know thee who alone art truly God, and Jesus Christ whom thou hast sent.'

The last word is a warning to be on the watch against *false gods* (idols, in the Greek). One would not have thought these rather sophisticated, Greek-minded readers would have been tempted to worship idols, but perhaps the writer is making his final thrust like this: Keep clear of false beliefs, he says, because if you do not you may as well go back to worshipping 'gods of wood and stone'. Perhaps there is a distant echo of the words of Joshua just before the fall of Jericho, 'keep yourselves from the devoted thing', i.e. do not loot, because the city is to be God's property (Josh. 6: 18). ✳

THE SECOND LETTER OF JOHN

(For the background to this letter see pp. 11, 12 and 13–16)

Truth and Love

A GREETING WITH A HIDDEN MEANING

1 THE ELDER to the Lady chosen by God, and her children, whom I love in truth—and not I alone but all
2 who know the truth—for the sake of the truth that dwells among us and will be with us for ever.

3   Grace, mercy, and peace shall be with us from God the Father and from Jesus Christ the Son of the Father, in truth and love.

✳ As is plain when the reader looks at pp. 400 and 401 in the small edition of the N.E.B., this letter and the so-called Third Letter of John are almost exactly of equal length, and there is a marked similarity between the opening paragraph of each letter and the closing paragraph. On the other hand the Second Letter is general in tone, mentioning no individual persons other than the writer, while the Third Letter mentions three, Gaius, Diotrephes and Demetrius, and describes concrete situations with great vividness.

The opening here begins (like 3 John) with the words *The elder to*. The Greek word is *ho presbuteros*. For some possible meanings of this phrase see p. 15. Briefly, it must have referred to someone who could be identified by the phrase *the elder*, but we do not know whether this was someone widely known through the church in those parts as 'the elder' or just 'the elder' to them, nor whether *elder* here is a matter of age or authority. More important, at this point in the commentary, is to discover what is meant by *the Lady chosen by God* (verse 1), the recipient, with her children, of the letter. There is strong reason to think that *the Lady* is a personification of some local church congregation. The writer announces his love for her and her children, but says that he loves them *in truth*. This means more than that 'he truly loves them' for in the next line he says that *all who know the truth* share this love for them. This suggests that when he says he loves them *in truth* he means he loves them as those who share his understanding of the truth. It would be extraordinary if one individual woman and her family could be said to be loved by *all who know the truth* but this phrase could apply to a congregation of good standing in the primitive church. A final piece of evidence is supplied by verse 13, where it emerges that the letter brings greetings from the children of the recipient's sister. These, like the Lady and her children, are described as *chosen by God*. Clearly we are dealing with a letter to a church, from a writer who is situated, either permanently or temporarily, in another church. In 1 Pet. 5: 13 we read, 'Greetings from her who dwells in Babylon, chosen by God like you'; this is another case where a church is referred to by a feminine pronoun, 'her'.

He says that he loves them *for the sake of the truth* (verse 2) and claims that this truth is among them and will remain so for ever. He speaks of this permanent possession of the truth in language that recalls the words of Jesus in John 14: 15, 16 about the Holy Spirit: 'I will ask the Father, and he will give you another to be your Advocate, who will be with you for ever—the Spirit of truth.'

The greeting in verse 3 is unusual because it does not so much express a wish as state a fact—grace, mercy and peace (the same trio as in 1 Tim. 1: 2 and 2 Tim. 1: 2) shall be with them. Notice the 'bracketing' of Jesus Christ with God the

Father as equally with him the source of blessings, and notice the phrase *the Son of the Father* which occurs in this form only here in the New Testament. It is used in the ancient hymn (see Book of Common Prayer) 'Glory be to God on high'— 'O Lord God, Lamb of God, Son of the Father'. This hymn may go back to the second century. ✻

TRUTH AND LOVE

4 I was delighted to find that some of your children are living by the truth, as we were commanded by the Father.
5 And now I have a request to make of you. Do not think I am giving a new command; I am recalling the one we have had before us from the beginning: let us love one
6 another. And love means following the commands of God. This is the command which was given you from the beginning, to be your rule of life.

✻ Having mentioned 'truth and love' in verse 3, the writer says that some of his readers' *children* (i.e. some members of the church to which he is writing) are 'walking' or living *by the truth*, and he calls on them also to walk in love—*let us love one another* (verse 5). This part of the letter is almost exactly a replica of points in 1 John, especially in 1 John 1: 7 and 4: 7. Detailed comment is unnecessary. The N.E.B. phrase in verse 6, *to be your rule of life*, is an interesting rendering of the Greek, which literally is 'so that you should walk by it', i.e. by the command that they had had from the start. 'Rule of life' has a modern ecclesiastical flavour perhaps not quite suitable to a document of this early date. ✻

THE FALSE TEACHERS AND HOW TO
DEAL WITH THEM

7 Many deceivers have gone out into the world, who do not acknowledge Jesus Christ as coming in the flesh. These

are the persons described as the Antichrist, the arch-
deceiver. Beware of them, so that you may not lose all 8
that we worked for, but receive your reward in full.

Anyone who runs ahead too far, and does not stand by 9
the doctrine of the Christ, is without God; he who stands
by that doctrine possesses both the Father and the Son.
If anyone comes to you who does not bring this doctrine, 10
do not welcome him into your house or give him a
greeting; for anyone who gives him a greeting is an 11
accomplice in his wicked deeds.

✳ Verse 7 repeats for this church the same charge about *deceivers* as we read in 1 John 2: 18, 19; 1 John 4: 1–3 and elsewhere. The Greek in verse 7 is rightly translated *coming* (i.e. in
the future) but the writer's meaning was almost certainly the
same as that in 1 John 4: 2, the point at issue being whether or
not Jesus *had* come in the past, not whether he would so come
in the future. Verse 7 is curiously expressed in the Greek. It
says: 'Many deceivers went out into the world, those who did
not acknowledge Jesus Christ coming [or having come, as
was probably meant] in flesh. *This man* is the deceiver and
the Antichrist.' Presumably the writer wants to say that in the
manifold teachers of wrong doctrine there can be seen the
activity of the one arch-deceiver, but he *could* mean—'do not
look for a single arch-deceiver; the oft-repeated heresies are the
thing to beware of'.

In verses 9 and 10 he makes the same assertions as were
made in 1 John 2: 22, 23. To harbour wrong doctrine concerning the coming of Jesus in the flesh is to be deprived of the
supreme possession, it is to be *without God*. Here the special
type of error condemned is 'running ahead too far and not
standing by the doctrine of the Christ'. 'Running ahead' is
the N.E.B.'s rendering of the Greek word *proagō*. This is the
only case in the New Testament where this word is used in a
disparaging sense, but it is clearly linked here with the second

phrase. It is not 'pressing on' that is wrong, but pressing on in a way that separates from *the doctrine of the Christ*. The N.E.B. has come down in favour of *the doctrine of the Christ*. The Greek could mean simply 'Christ's teaching'.

Verses 10 and 11 command the readers to boycott any travelling missionaries who arrive without the true teaching. They are not to be received, not even greeted. The fear of contamination by false doctrine was very great. 'John the disciple of the Lord' as we saw (p. 10) is said to have fled from a bath-house because he found the heretic Cerinthus was inside too. Conversely, the importance of welcoming and greeting true fellow-Christians travelling on their 'lawful occasions' or on special Christian missions was often stressed (see, e.g. 3 John 5). *

WAITING FOR A FACE-TO-FACE MEETING

12 I have much to write to you, but I do not care to put it down in black and white. But I hope to visit you and talk with you face to face, so that our joy may be complete.

13 The children of your Sister, chosen by God, send their greetings.

* The letter is ended almost in the same words as 3 John. He will not write *in black and white* (literally, 'with paper and ink'; it is difficult to see why the N.E.B. paraphrased). He looks forward to a personal meeting. *The children of your Sister, chosen by God* clearly means the membership of the church where the writer is resident. Whether this was his home church or not, it is impossible to say. The writer appears to speak with some authority to a church other than his own, as if he had a general superintendency over an area. One scholar once expressed this by suggesting that the church had archbishops before it had bishops! *

THE THIRD LETTER OF JOHN

(For the background to this letter see pp. 12–16)

Trouble in the Church

A WARM GREETING FOR GAIUS

THE ELDER to dear Gaius, whom I love in truth.   1
My dear Gaius, I pray that you may enjoy good 2
health, and that all may go well with you, as I know it
goes well with your soul. I was delighted when friends 3
came and told me how true you have been; indeed you
are true in your whole life. Nothing gives me greater joy 4
than to hear that my children are living by the truth.

* This is the only letter of the three which is addressed to a
named person, and the person is *Gaius*. Nothing is known of
him apart from what can be deduced about him from this
letter. There is no reason to identify him with the Gaius of
Rom. 16: 23, Paul's host in Corinth, who had been baptized
by Paul (1 Cor. 1: 14). *That* Gaius was possibly the same as
the one mentioned in Acts 19: 29 as a travelling companion of
Paul and who may appear again in Acts 20: 4 ('Gaius the
Doberian' as in the N.E.B., not 'Gaius of Derbe' as in the
R.V.). It would not be impossible for the Gaius of Acts 20: 4
to be the Gaius of 3 John 1, if for some reason he had settled in
Asia, but there is no reason to assume this. It was a common
name. A later tradition (fourth century) says that John or-
dained him as bishop of Pergamon (on the west coast of Asia
Minor), but again there is no known evidence to support
this tradition.

The writer is described as *the elder*, just as at the beginning
of 2 John. In view of other close similarities, particularly in

the ending, it may be assumed that the writer is the writer of
2 John. For what can be confidently asserted about him, see
pp. 14 and 15.

The writer loves Gaius *in truth* (verse 1) as he does also 'the
Lady chosen by God' (2 John 1) and once more this probably
means that he loves him as a fellow-believer in the truth as
Jesus has made it known. *My dear Gaius* of the N.E.B. in
verse 2 is a rather free rendering of the Greek word *agapēte*
'beloved'. The writer prays that Gaius may have good health
and that things will go well with him, as is the case with his
soul. The Greek word for soul is *psyche*, which does not usually
convey the *spiritual* atmosphere of the English word *soul*. For
this we expect the Greek word *pneuma*. The context seems,
however, to demand this translation into English. The writer
has had friends arriving with good news concerning Gaius's
attitude to 'the truth'. This brings particular joy to the writer,
who seems to include Gaius among his *children* (verse 4). This
suggests that Gaius had become a Christian through the
missionary work of the writer of the letter. ✷

HELP FOR TRAVELLING MISSIONARIES—RECEIVED AND HOPED FOR

5 My dear friend, you show a fine loyalty in everything
that you do for these our fellow-Christians, strangers
6 though they are to you. They have spoken of your kindness before the congregation here. Please help them on
7 their journey in a manner worthy of the God we serve. It
was on Christ's work that they went out; and they would
8 accept nothing from pagans. We are bound to support
such men, and so play our part in spreading the truth.

✷ Now we have more detail about the good report the writer
has received about Gaius. In particular he has loyally helped
certain fellow-Christians ('brothers' in the Greek). This story

has been told by those who benefited from Gaius's kind hospitality and assistance for their journey. Now, however, they seem to have set off from the writer's base again, perhaps to go further afield, for Gaius is asked once more to *help them on their journey* (verse 6). They had set out it is said *on Christ's work* (verse 7)—a very free translation of the Greek, which says 'they went out for the sake of the Name'. This probably means 'they went out as missionaries, preaching the Name of Christ', but it *could* mean 'they went out', i.e. were driven out, 'because they were faithful to the traditional, orthodox faith of the church in Christ as the Name for our salvation'. These missionaries had refused to accept help from pagans. There was some tradition in the early Church that missionaries must be very careful not to be a burden on those they sought to evangelize (e.g. 1 Thess. 2: 9, 'We worked for a living night and day, rather than be a burden to anyone, while we proclaimed before you the good news of God', and *Didache* 11: 6, where a travelling missionary is said to be no true prophet if he stays for three days !). But these passages do not provide an exact parallel with the elder's thought in this passage. ✻

DIOTREPHES VERSUS THE ELDER

I sent a letter to the congregation, but Diotrephes, their 9 would-be leader, will have nothing to do with us. If I 10 come, I will bring up the things he is doing. He lays base- less and spiteful charges against us; not satisfied with that, he refuses to receive our friends, and he interferes with those who would do so, and tries to expel them from the congregation.

✻ These few lines give us more information about the life of the primitive church than all the rest of the Johannine letters put together. Yet the information they give is tantalizingly inadequate.

What is the situation envisaged in these lines? The elder has
sent a letter *to the congregation* ('church' in the old versions).
Apparently this letter made a request and the only request
actually implied is that the church should receive the elder's
friends (verse 10). It would be tempting to think that the
unfruitful letter is our 2 John. It is addressed to a church; it
begins and ends much as does 3 John; it is almost exactly the
same length—one could imagine that the elder had two
identical sheets of papyrus, filled them both, and sent one to
Gaius and one to the church. It is not absolutely certain that
the letter to the church *preceded* the letter to Gaius—the letters
could have gone 'by the same post'. The unfortunate events
of verse 10 would then be an account of the general behaviour
of Diotrephes and those whom he controlled, behaviour
which would make rejection of a simultaneous letter almost
certain.

It must be said that 2 John does not make a request for a
good reception of orthodox missionaries: only a warning
against receiving unorthodox ones.

What of Diotrephes? Nothing more is known of him than
appears in this sentence. The N.E.B. calls him *their would-be
leader* (verse 9). The Greek is 'their loving-to-take-the-lead
Diotrephes'. Was this just a case of a wilful dominating man,
who resented the leadership of the elder, especially when
exercised from a distance? Or does the sentence conceal the
first clearly recorded case of a man ruling a church as a single
('monarchical'—'monarch-like') bishop? And is it significant
that the writer, who cannot persuade him, happens to be an
'elder', the rank from which bishops may sometimes have
emerged? And did Gaius live near the church of Diotrephes?
—was 'the church' Gaius's church? Was he one who had
been 'expelled' (verse 10) just because he received the emissaries of the elder? And was this a personal quarrel, or a
dispute over forms of government? Or did it have anything
to do with beliefs—those of the elder, and those of Diotrephes?
If we knew the answers to these questions we should know a

great deal more than we do about a mysterious chapter in early Church history. All we can say is that beliefs, and the practices based on them, are fundamental to 1 John and 2 John. It seems strange if they are quite irrelevant to 3 John, which is obviously so closely linked to the other letters, particularly to 2 John. *

BEHAVIOUR AND ITS BEARING ON RELATIONSHIPS WITH GOD

My dear friend, do not imitate bad examples, but good 11 ones. The well-doer is a child of God; the evil-doer has never seen God.

* This short sentence links the *moral* teaching of the letter to 1 John, especially to 1 John 3: 4-6, and 9, where we find both the ideas of 3 John 11. 1 John 3: 6, 'the sinner has not *seen* him'; 1 John 3: 9, 'a *child* of God does not commit sin'. The 'bad examples' are apparently those of Diotrephes and people like him; the 'good ones' those of men like Demetrius (verse 12). *

THE GOOD REPUTATION OF DEMETRIUS

Demetrius gets a good testimonial from everybody—yes, 12 and from the truth itself. I add my testimony, and you know that my testimony is true.

* Here is another character, Demetrius, otherwise unknown. He *may* have been the bearer of the letter. The most interesting phrase here is *from the truth itself*. How can 'the truth' give Demetrius a good testimonial? Now it so happens that Papias, bishop of Hierapolis, about A.D. 140, uses an almost identical phrase (see p. 6). He says (according to Irenaeus, quoted by Eusebius) that he took delight in those who recall the commandments given by the Lord to faith, and reaching us 'from the truth itself'. Of course Papias may be recalling

the phrase of the elder in his letter—he refers to 'John the elder', a few lines down the page. But he may be using 'the truth' as a kind of metaphor for the whole orthodox tradition. If this is so, possibly our writer is doing something similar. Demetrius gets his testimonial 'from the whole active community of those animated by the truth'. This, though strange, seems more likely than those theories which identify 'the truth' with Christ, or the Holy Spirit, though we cannot forget that Jesus in the Fourth Gospel calls himself 'the truth' (John 14: 6) and that in 1 John 5: 6 we find *the Spirit is truth* (literally, 'the truth'). ✳

HOPE OF A PERSONAL MEETING

13 I have much to write to you, but I do not care to set it
14 down with pen and ink. I hope to see you very soon, and we will talk face to face. Peace be with you. Our friends send their greetings. Greet our friends individually.

✳ The elder ends the letter in almost precisely the same words as were used to end 2 John. He will not write more; he will await a personal meeting; it is just like the endings we ourselves use. 'No more now; all the news when we meet.' But notice a subtle variation. Here he says he will not set down his news *with pen and ink* (verse 13). There he said 'paper and ink' (2 John 12)—'black and white' according to the free translation of the N.E.B. A forger, imitating 2 John in 3 John, or 3 John in 2 John, would have more probably used the same expression, not one that is very similar, but subtly different.

Greet our friends individually. The Greek has *by name*, but this was a common phrase meaning 'one by one'. It seems to suggest that the greetings were not likely to be acceptable to the Church as a whole, but that the writer had a number of friends who would welcome his message. ✳

✳ ✳ ✳ ✳ ✳ ✳ ✳ ✳ ✳ ✳ ✳ ✳ ✳

A LETTER OF JAMES

A LETTER OF
JAMES

✳　✳　✳　✳　✳　✳　✳　✳　✳　✳　✳　✳　✳

THE MEN CALLED JAMES IN THE NEW TESTAMENT

One of the obviously important and interesting questions that
will have to be discussed later is who wrote the book headed
in the N.E.B. 'A Letter of James'. Before we embark on that
matter, however, it is necessary to sort out the various people
called James in the New Testament. There are at least three
of these, and although with the aid of a concordance anyone
could work out this problem on his own, it will probably save
a lot of time and trouble to have the information set out clearly
at the beginning of this section of the book.

The word *James* comes to us from the Greek *Jakōbos*,
through the Italian form *Giacomo*. There are three people who
seem to bear this name in the New Testament, though some
traditions have identified James 2 (as we shall call him) with
James 3, thereby reducing the number to two, and some have
thought that James 2 is really two people, not one, thereby
making a possible four in all.

The three principal figures are:

(*a*) James 1, the son of Zebedee;
(*b*) James 2, the son of Alphaeus;
(*c*) James 3, the brother of Jesus.

James 1. He first appears in the Gospel story at Mark 1: 19
('when he had gone a little further he saw James son of Zebedee
and his brother John, who were in the boat overhauling their
nets. He called them; and leaving their father Zebedee in the
boat with the hired men, they went off to follow him'). He
seems to be the older, or slightly more important of the

second pair of fishermen-brothers to be called to the life of discipleship by Jesus, the former pair being Andrew and Peter (Mark 1: 16, 17). The same story is told in Matt. 4: 18–22, and, in a rather different form (if it is agreed that the same incident is being described), in Luke 5: 1–11.

This James always appears in the lists of the apostles (Matt. 10: 2; Mark 3: 14; Luke 6: 15; Acts 1: 13) and always among the first four names, Peter, John and Andrew being listed with him. Peter always heads the list, but Andrew, Peter's brother, can appear as no. 2 with Peter, or after James and John. These always appear together in the formal lists, and except in Acts (1: 13) James precedes John.

In the Gospel narrative, it is a trio ('Peter and James and John') not a quartet (the same, with Andrew added) who are picked out for a specially close intimacy with Jesus. They follow him into the house of Jairus for the raising of his daughter (Mark 5: 37) and also to the mountain of the Transfiguration (Mark 9: 2) and into the recesses of the Garden of Gethsemane where the darker moments of the Agony were to take place (Mark 14: 33). James and John were called Boanerges (Sons of Thunder) as we are told in Mark 3: 17, possibly because they wanted to call down fire from heaven to burn up Samaritans who would not receive Jesus and his friends (Luke 9: 53). These two were of course the sons of Zebedee who asked for the favour of sitting in state on the right and left hand of Jesus (Mark 10: 35–40).

Provided that all the names and relationships of the friends and relations of Jesus are accurately stated in the Gospels and letters of the New Testament, certain further identifications can be made. Mark 15: 40 lists the following women as present at the cross, 'watching from a distance'—'Mary of Magdala, Mary the mother of James the younger and of Joseph, and Salome'. In the corresponding passage in Matt. 27: 56 we read, 'Mary of Magdala, Mary the mother of James and Joseph, and the mother of the sons of Zebedee'. According to Matthew, then, the mother of the sons of Zebedee was called Salome. Going further, we learn from John 19: 25 on one interpretation that there were three 'Mary's' at the cross— the mother of Jesus, 'with her sister, Mary wife of Clopas, and Mary of Magdala'. The second Mary (wife of Clopas) *can* be identified with the sister of Mary the mother of Jesus (although there would hardly be two 'Mary's' in one family). But there are a number of ambiguities disguised in the English version of the N.E.B. In the first place *wife of Clopas* translates a Greek phrase saying 'the one [feminine] of Clopas', and this *could* mean the *daughter* of Clopas, in which case it *could* mean that Jesus' mother was the daughter of Clopas, and Mary Magdalene her sister, there being only two women altogether. For various reasons this is wildly improbable. But the whole phrase could describe *four* women—Jesus' mother, her sister (both unnamed), Mary of Clopas, and Mary Magdalene. It has been necessary to describe the many possible interpretations of this verse for reasons which will appear later.

To complete the story of James the son of Zebedee it is only necessary to say that he was one of the apostolic band in Acts 1: 13, and that he was martyred under Herod Agrippa I, about A.D. 44 (see Acts 12: 2).

James 2. This is to be our shorthand description of 'James the less' as he is often called. He first appears in Mark 3: 18 as 'James the son of Alphaeus', number 9 in the list of apostles (similarly in Matthew and Luke). Luke (6: 16) has an apostle called *Judas son of James*, but again 'son of' is one of two alternative translations; it could be 'brother of'—all the Greek has is *Judas of James*. James 2 is usually identified with *James the younger* of Mark 15: 40 who comes in there as a son, with Joseph, of a certain Mary—probably the 'Clopas's Mary' of John 19: 25. The Greek phrase is *James the little (ho mikros)*, but the N.E.B. may be right in saying *James the younger*. This James disappears from the New Testament history after being named in Acts 1: 13 *unless* he is the James referred to in Jude 1, where Jude calls himself *brother of James*. This is not probable: see below.

James 3. This is *James the Lord's brother*, the traditionally accepted author of 'The Letter of James'. It is convenient to start studying his story from Gal. 1: 19. Here Paul, writing at some time around A.D. 50, refers to this James as being in an important position in relation to the church in Jerusalem. He saw him on the visit when he first visited Peter (Cephas) (Gal. 1: 18, 19). He saw him 'fourteen years later' (Gal. 2: 1 and Gal. 2: 9). He became aware of his influence again when 'certain persons came from James' to Antioch (Gal. 2: 12). Most of these incidents certainly occurred long after the martyr-death of James the Apostle, and in any case this James (James 3) is described as 'the Lord's brother'.

Going back to the Gospels we find in Mark 3: 31 ff. that the mother of Jesus 'and his brothers' arrived where Jesus was teaching, and apparently tried to restrain him in his public work (cf. Mark 3: 20, 21). Mark 6: 3 is more important. Here, in his home town his audience say 'How does he work such miracles? Is not this the carpenter, the son of Mary, the brother of James and Joseph and Judas and Simon? And are not his sisters here with us?' So long as words are given their natural meaning, this implies that Jesus had a brother named James, and he was almost certainly the eldest of a family born to Mary and Joseph after the birth of Jesus.

As we shall see, by no means all Christian scholars in ancient or modern times have been able to believe that the mother of Jesus had any other children after giving birth to Jesus, but assuming that she did, and that James 3 was among them, let us follow out his subsequent history as far as we can.

There is no evidence that he became a believer in or follower of Jesus before the crucifixion, although it is equally true to say there is no evidence that he did not. What we do know, according to 1 Cor. 15: 7, is that Jesus appeared to James after the resurrection. This was an appearance which had some special character, for it is distinguished from appearances to Peter, the Twelve, 'five hundred brothers at once', and 'all the apostles' whatever that means. Early tradition believed that this vision was in response to some expression on James's part that he would not eat 'from the hour in which he had drunk the cup of the Lord' until he saw Jesus risen from the dead. This story, which seemed to assume (quite wrongly) that James was at the Last Supper, comes from 'the Gospel according to the Hebrews', one of the more respectable of the 'apocryphal' gospels (gospels not accepted as authoritative). It is quoted by Jerome in A.D. 392. There are other forms of the story. Whether they are of real historical importance it is difficult to say. They could easily have arisen from a desire to explain how James 'the Lord's brother' became a follower of Jesus, and eventually a key figure in the church of Jerusalem.

Coming back now to the period after the resurrection, we find James (and it must be 'our James') in a leading position in Jerusalem. Acts 12: 17 shows how Peter, on escape from prison said at once, 'Report this to James and the members of the church'. At an important conference dealing with the conditions under which Gentiles could enter the Church, James appears as a kind of chairman or moderator (see Acts 15: 13, 'James summed up'). Later, when Paul arrived at Jerusalem on what proved to be his last visit, he paid a visit to James the day after his arrival (Acts 21: 18). At that meeting, he was advised (not necessarily by James, but very probably so) to join a group of Jews who were going through a ritual vow, in order to allay fears that he and his friends were against the Jewish law.

That is the end of the story as far as the New Testament is concerned, but early writers outside the Bible give us a great deal more information.

Josephus, the renegade Jew, who joined the Romans, but wrote important books of Jewish history, wrote of James in A.D. 96 (in *Antiquities*, 20: 9. 1) as follows:

'During the interval between the death of Festus (A.D. 62) and the arrival of his successor Albinus, the high priest Ananus the younger, being of a rash and daring spirit, and inclined like the Sadducees to general severity in punishing, brought to trial James the brother of Jesus, who is called the Christ, and some others before the court of the Sanhedrin, and having charged them with breaking the laws, delivered them over to be stoned. The better class of citizens, and those who were versed in the laws were indignant at this, and made complaints both to King Agrippa and to Albinus, on the ground that Ananus had no right to summon the Sanhedrin without the consent of the procurator; and Agrippa in consequence removed him from the high priesthood.'

Very important information about James the Lord's brother is given in the second book of Eusebius's *Ecclesiastical History* (written A.D. 325) in the first and twenty-third chapters of that work.

In the first chapter Eusebius says, 'James whom the ancients surnamed the Just, on account of the excellence of his virtue, is recorded to have been the first to be made bishop of the church of Jerusalem'. He goes on to state that he was called the brother of the Lord because he was known as a son of Joseph. He quotes Clement of Alexandria (*c.* A.D. 200) as saying in his book *Outlines* (no longer extant) that 'Peter and James and John...strove not after honour, but chose James the Just bishop of Jerusalem'. Clement is also stated to have said elsewhere that 'the Lord after his resurrection imparted knowledge to James the Just and to John and Peter', who passed it on to the other disciples and to the seventy. In this passage it looks as though Clement has confused James 3 with James 1, but he quickly adds 'there were two Jameses, one called the Just, who was thrown from the pinnacle of the temple, and was beaten to death with a club by a fuller, and another who was beheaded'. Clement in any case treats James 3 and James 2 as the same person, for he says 'there were *two* Jameses'.

In chapter 23 of Book II Eusebius deals more fully with the martyrdom of James the Just. He begins with a summary in his own words. The Jews, he says, failed to capture Paul, who escaped them by appealing to Caesar; so in their anger they turned against James. They demanded that he should publicly renounce Christ. On the contrary, he boldly and clearly announced his faith in him as saviour and Son of God. Because of his great reputation for asceticism and piety this public witness enraged them, and they slew him by throwing him from the temple, and beating him with a club.

Eusebius then tells the story in detail, as he found it in Hegesippus (a second-century church historian). This passage, though it contains much that cannot easily be believed, is so important that much of it must be quoted in full.

'James, the brother of the Lord, succeeded to the government of the church in conjunction with the apostles. He has been called the Just by all from the time of our Saviour to the present day; for there were many that bore the name of James. He was holy from his mother's womb; and he drank no wine nor strong drink, nor did he eat flesh. No razor came upon his head; he did not anoint himself with oil, and he did not use the bath. He alone was permitted to enter the holy place; for he wore not woollen but linen garments. And he was in the habit of entering alone into the temple and was frequently found upon his knees begging forgiveness for the people, so that his knees became hard like those of a camel, in consequence of his constantly bending them in his worship of God, and asking forgiveness for the people. Because of his exceeding great justice he was called the Just, and Oblias, which signified in Greek [surely Hegesippus meant *Hebrew*!] *Bulwark of the people* and *Justice* in accordance with what the prophets declare of him. Now some of the seven sects [Hegesippus means Jewish sects, which he describes elsewhere] ...asked him, "What is the gate of Jesus?" [Presumably they meant, "What does faith in Jesus lead to?"] and he replied that he was the Saviour.'

The story then becomes extremely far-fetched. Some believed because of James's testimony, whereupon the majority insisted on James standing on a pinnacle of the temple publicly to denounce Christ. When he was up there he did the opposite, proclaiming almost in the words of Jesus at his trial, that the Son of Man was about to come in power. This greatly enraged the Jewish leaders, who cried out, 'The just man is also in error'. They fulfilled, we read, Isaiah's words, 'Let us take away the just man because he is troublesome to us'. They threw him down, then stoned him. Like Stephen, he died praying for his murderers. He was finally finished by a blow from a fuller with a club (as Clement also said).

A great deal of this is clearly legendary. James has been built up into a *Jewish* rather than a Christian saint, except in the cause and manner of his death. It is quite impossible to say what basis of fact lies behind all this, but if we take Clement, Hegesippus, and Josephus together, and put their evidence alongside what comes out in Galatians and Acts we can discern: (1) a figure called James, a brother of Jesus, leading the church at Jerusalem; (2) a man who stood closer to the old Jewish religion than most of the leaders of the Christian Church, and who retained a good deal of the respect and affection of the Jews; (3) one who finally suffered as a martyr in spite of his old-fashioned piety.

It is convenient to mention now the ending of this famous chapter from Eusebius.

'These things are recorded in regard to James who is said to be the author of the first of the so-called catholic epistles [our "letter of James"]. But it is to be observed that it is disputed; at least not many of the ancients have mentioned it, as is the case likewise with the epistle that bears the name of Jude, which is also one of the seven so-called catholic epistles. Nevertheless, we know that these also, with the rest, have been read publicly in very many churches'.

What does the word *brother* mean? From Galatians onwards we have found constant references to James as 'the brother of the Lord'.

We have seen that this originally appeared to mean *brother* in the ordinary sense, i.e. that James and Jesus had the same mother. But from the time of Jerome (a great scholar of the

fourth century, who wrote and taught both at Rome and in
Bethlehem) there have been those who followed Jerome in
believing that the word 'brother' in this context means not
brother in our sense, but *cousin* or 'kinsman'. This view was
based on the idea that 'James the Lord's brother' was the same
person as 'James the son of Alphaeus' (i.e. that James 2 and
James 3 were the same man). To support this idea, Jerome
pointed out that in Gal. 1: 18, 19 James the Lord's brother is
called an apostle. ('I stayed with him', i.e. Peter '...without
seeing any other of the apostles, except James the Lord's
brother'.) Jerome's argument runs: James the Lord's brother
was an apostle. He must therefore have been James the son of
Alphaeus (see Mark 3: 18). But there was a Mary the mother
of James the younger (Mark 15: 40) who, Jerome thinks, was
identical with Mary of Clopas (John 19: 25) and who was, in
his view, sister of Mary the mother of Jesus. James therefore,
James the younger, James the son of Alphaeus, was in Jerome's
eyes, the son of the sister of Jesus' mother, was his cousin, and
therefore was called 'brother', meaning relative or kinsman.

This view was the opposite of that held by another fourth-
century writer, Helvidius, and he taught what most modern
scholars believe, namely that James the Lord's brother was a
real brother of Jesus. The main arguments in favour of this
view are: It is the natural meaning of all the language used in
the New Testament. It is not necessary to interpret Gal. 1: 19
in such a way as to think James the Lord's brother was an
apostle in the sense of being 'one of the Twelve'. It is *not*
likely that Mary of Clopas was the sister of Mary the mother
of Jesus. To have two sisters of the same name is improbable
in any case, and all the 'family trees' work out better if
Salome, the mother of the sons of Zebedee, is taken as the
sister of Jesus' mother in the difficult text, John 19: 25.

So far we have been getting the information about the
various 'Jameses' into order. We still have to examine the
probability or otherwise of 'James 3' being the author of the
letter bearing his name.

It is particularly important to study the relationship between
'James' and other books in the New Testament, for the
questions of when the book was written, and by whom,
largely turn upon this.

It is plain to all readers that the subject-matter of the Letter
of James stands in particularly close relationship to the teaching of Jesus in the Synoptic Gospels. As we read James, we
are reminded again and again of the Sermon on the Mount.
Many verses in James are particularly close to the teaching
of Jesus as recorded in Matthew. To make this clear a few
examples are set out in parallel columns.

JAMES	MATTHEW
My brothers, whenever you have to face trials of many kinds, count yourselves supremely happy (1: 2).	How blest you are, when you suffer insults and persecution and every kind of calumny for my sake. Accept it with gladness (5: 11, 12).
If any of you falls short in wisdom, he should ask God for it and it will be given him (1: 5).	Ask, and you will receive (7: 7).
But each of you must be quick to listen, slow to speak, and slow to be angry (1: 19).	Anyone who nurses anger against his brother must be brought to judgement (5: 22).
Only be sure that you act on the message and do not merely listen (1: 22).	What then of the man who hears these words of mine and acts upon them? (7: 24, cf. 7: 26).
For if a man keeps the whole	If any man therefore sets

JAMES   MATTHEW

law apart from one single point, he is guilty of breaking all of it (2: 10).

aside even the least of the Law's demands, and teaches others to do the same, he will have the lowest place in the kingdom of Heaven...(5: 19).

In that judgement there will be no mercy for the man who has shown no mercy (2: 13).

How blest are those who show mercy; mercy shall be shown to them (5: 7).

True justice is the harvest reaped by peacemakers from seeds sown in a spirit of peace (3: 18).

How blest are the peacemakers; God shall call them his sons (5: 9).

Have you never learned that love of the world is enmity to God? (4: 4).

No servant can be slave to two masters; for either he will hate the first and love the second, or he will be devoted to the first and think nothing of the second. You cannot serve God and Money (6: 24).

Humble yourselves before God and he will lift you high (4: 10).

How blest are those of a gentle spirit; they shall have the earth for their possession (5: 5).

He who disparages a brother or passes judgement on his brother disparages the law and judges the law (4: 11).

Pass no judgement, and you will not be judged (7: 1).

Your riches have rotted; your fine clothes are moth-eaten;

Store up treasure in heaven, where there is no moth and

JAMES	MATTHEW
your silver and gold have rusted away...(5: 2, 3).	no rust to spoil it, no thieves to break in and steal (6: 20).
Above all things, my brothers, do not use oaths, whether 'by heaven' or 'by earth' or by anything else. When you say yes or no, let it be plain 'Yes' or 'No', for fear that you expose yourselves to judgement (5: 12).	But what I tell you is this: You are not to swear at all —not by heaven, for it is God's throne, nor by earth, for it is his footstool, nor by Jerusalem, for it is the city of the great King.... Plain 'Yes' or 'No' is all you need to say; anything beyond that comes from the devil (5: 34-7).

There is clearly *some* link between what is to be found in James, and in Matthew, particularly in the Sermon on the Mount. There is no other New Testament book (apart of course from Luke), where there are so many distinct echoes of the Sermon on the Mount. Yet it is noticeable that in no case do we find *exact* repetitions in James of sentences in Matthew. The last instance quoted (Jas. 5: 12—Matt. 5: 34-7) is the closest parallel. It does not look as if 'James' was actually quoting from the book Matthew. What does look probable is that they were both familiar with a section of Christ's teaching that had been handed down for a time mainly in oral form. This would explain the distinct similarities, and also the obvious divergencies.

What is more important than the exact literary history of the two documents is the fact that James has a *point of view* so similar to that which marks the teaching of Jesus *during his lifetime*. Much of James reads like the gospel *of* Jesus rather than the gospel *about* Jesus.

The references to Jesus are remarkably few in James. There is the opening sentence, 'From James, a servant of God and the

Lord Jesus Christ' (1: 1). There is 2: 1, 'My brothers, believing as you do in our Lord Jesus Christ, who reigns in glory,
you must never show snobbery'. And there is 5: 7, 'Be patient,
my brothers, until the Lord comes', which can hardly be anything other than a reference to the second coming of Christ.
If it were not for these brief references (especially 2: 1) much
of James could have been made up of discourses for the
disciples to use, even during their apostolic tours (that is, before the crucifixion). This is not a serious possibility, but it
shows that the type of Christianity involved retains very
primitive features—either because the letter was written at an
early date (e.g. about A.D. 45) or because a form of Christianity
with a primitive theology had survived in some obscure corner
of the Christian world, just as it did in those circles which
produced the *Didache* ('The Teaching of the Twelve Apostles',
a Christian handbook of early but uncertain date).

Then there are links between James and 1 Peter which
must be noted.

JAMES	I PETER
Greetings to the Twelve Tribes dispersed throughout the world (1: 1).	...to those of God's scattered people who lodge for a while in Pontus, Galatia, Cappadocia, Asia, and Bithynia (1: 1).
My brothers, whenever you have to face trials of many kinds, count yourselves supremely happy, in the knowledge that such testing of your faith breeds fortitude, and if you give fortitude full play you will go on to complete a balanced character that will fall short in nothing (1: 2–4).	This is cause for great joy, even though now you smart for a little while, if need be, under trials of many kinds. Even gold passes through the assayer's fire, and more precious than perishable gold is faith which has stood the test (1: 6, 7).

JAMES

I PETER

Happy the man who remains steadfast under trial, for having passed that test he will receive for his prize the gift of life promised to those who love God (1: 12).

Of his set purpose, by declaring the truth, he gave us birth to be a kind of first-fruits of his creatures (1: 18).

And then, when the Head Shepherd appears, you will receive for your own the unfading garland of glory (5: 4).

Praise be to the God and Father of our Lord Jesus Christ, who in his mercy gave us new birth into a living hope...(1: 3)

and

You have been born anew, not of mortal parentage but of immortal, through the living and enduring word of God (1: 23).

Away then with all that is sordid, and the malice that hurries to excess, and quietly accept the message planted in your hearts, which can bring you salvation (1: 21).

Then away with all malice and deceit, away with all pretence and jealousy and recrimination of every kind! Like the new-born infants you are, you must crave for pure milk (spiritual milk, I mean), so that you may thrive upon it to your souls' health (2: 1, 2).

Who among you is wise or clever? Let his right conduct give practical proof of it, with the modesty that comes of wisdom (3: 13).

...a gentle, quiet spirit, which is of high value in the sight of God (3: 4).

What causes conflicts and

...abstain from the lusts of

JAMES	I PETER
quarrels among you? Do they not spring from the aggressiveness of your bodily desires? (4: 1).	the flesh which are at war with the soul (2: 11).
...the grace he gives is stronger. Thus Scripture says, 'God opposes the arrogant and gives grace to the humble'. Be submissive then to God (4: 6, 7).	Indeed, all of you should wrap yourselves in the garment of humility towards each other, because God set his face against the arrogant but favours the humble. Humble yourselves then under God's mighty hand...(5: 5, 6).
Humble yourselves before God and he will lift you high (4: 10).	Humble yourselves then under God's mighty hand, and he will lift you up in due time (5: 6).

Some of these parallels are more striking in the Greek than in translation, particularly a free translation such as that in the N.E.B. Nevertheless, there are enough close parallels to make it probable that *either* the author of James knew 1 Peter or vice versa. Which of these suppositions is the truth is difficult to decide, and on it depends to some extent the probable date of James. It may suffice to say that J. B. Mayor, in his massive commentary, comes down in favour of the view that 1 Peter is based on James. It is a curious fact that apart from the references in 1 Pet. 5: 4, 1: 3, and 2: 11—see table above—the passages in both epistles with parallels in the other occur in the right order, i.e. it looks as though the author of one had the other before him, and worked little quotations from the other book into his own as he wrote it. It would not do to build too much on this but it is certainly interesting.

Nobody is quite sure when 1 Peter was written. If Peter

wrote it, it must have been written by about A.D. 62. If he did
not, it might be as late as A.D. 100. In any case the relationship
between James and 1 Peter, though close, is not clear enough to
allow any firm deductions about the date of either to be drawn.

We now come to the most important comparison of all—
that between James and Paul, especially between James and
the letters of Paul to the Galatians and the Romans. Here there
are very close parallels in the wording, but a sharp contrast in
the sentiments expressed.

The important passage in James is 2: 14–26. Here the writer
says that 'faith divorced from deeds is lifeless as a corpse'
(2: 26). In order to reach this conclusion he begins by mocking
at a charity consisting only in fine words (2: 16). Similarly,
he says, faith that does not lead to action is a lifeless thing. By
faith, he seems to mean a dry, intellectual belief—the devils
have this faith, he says, but it gives them no joy, it only makes
them tremble (2: 19).

Then in 2: 21 he claims that Abraham was justified by his
actions, when he was ready to offer Isaac on the altar. He
interprets the Old Testament text (Abraham 'believed in the
Lord; and he counted it to him for righteousness', Gen. 15: 6)
in that way. The faith, he says, was in the obedience. Later he
takes the friendly attitude of the prostitute Rahab to the
Israelite spies (2: 25; Josh. 2: 4, 15; 6: 17) as another example
of a *deed* that revealed faith.

Now much of this seems to lie in direct opposition to the
words of Paul. Whereas James says (2: 24), 'You see then that
a man is justified by deeds and not by faith in itself', Paul says
(Gal. 2: 16), 'We know that no man is ever justified by doing
what the law demands, but only through faith in Christ
Jesus'. Where James uses Abraham as an example of a man
justified by deeds, Paul uses him as an example of just the
opposite, a man justified by faith apart from deeds. In Rom. 4,
Paul devotes a long passage (the whole chapter, in our Bibles)
to proving that it was Abraham's faith and not his behaviour,
that led to his being 'declared righteous' or justified. He

quotes the very same verse as James (Gen. 15: 6): Abraham 'believed in the Lord; and he counted it to him for righteousness', but uses it in just the opposite way.

We need not at this moment discuss the relative truth or validity of the two views. The point now under consideration is which came first—Paul's letters to the Galatians and Romans, or James? If James used the Pauline letters, James has to be put after A.D. 60 and probably much later. It could only *just* be written by James the Lord's brother, for he was killed about A.D. 62 (see above, p. 77). If James is attacking not Paul's views, but a misunderstanding of them, the argument for a post-Pauline date is correspondingly stronger. But if Paul used James, the latter is firmly placed very early in the Christian era: it might be as early as A.D. 45. The similarity between its teaching and that of the teaching of Jesus in Matthew and Luke would then be easy to explain.

Forms of Jewish Christianity existed side by side with Gentile Christianity for many years. In this letter we have many of the *ideas* of Jewish Christians, expressed in the Greek language and in a style strongly influenced by a Hellenistic (late Greek) atmosphere.

THE USE OF JAMES IN THE EARLY CENTURIES OF THE CHURCH

We have seen that there are great similarities between certain passages in James and passages in Matthew, Romans, Galatians, and 1 Peter. Unfortunately in no case of a parallel is it possible to say with absolute certainty which writing influenced the other, or whether the similar phrases indicate familiarity with a common source or tradition. When one steps outside the canonical scriptures the first certain quotations or allusions are found in *The Shepherd of Hermas*, about A.D. 130 (an allegorical Christian 'romance').

In the *Muratorian Fragment*, a list of recognized scriptures dating from about A.D. 175, James does not occur, although

Jude, purporting to be by Jude the brother of James, does (Jude 1: 1).

Origen, the great scholar of Alexandria and Caesarea, refers pointedly to the letter, quoting Jas. 2: 20 with the words 'as we read in the epistle current as James's'. This passage occurs in Origen's commentary on John (19: 6) which appeared perhaps in A.D. 245.

The next clear landmark is Eusebius's *Ecclesiastical History*, written about A.D. 325 at Caesarea, on the coast of what is now called Israel. Eusebius in Book 3, chapter 25, says the writings of the New Testament could be divided into two groups, those which were 'true, genuine, and thoroughly acknowledged', and those which were ' " disputed", but nevertheless acknowledged by most of the church writers'. The 'disputed' group was further subdivided into those books which were just 'disputed' and those which he classed as definitely 'spurious'. James came into the better class of the disputed; with it were Jude, 2 Peter, and 2 and 3 John. These books built up the number of *general* or *catholic* letters to seven, a number which had a curious attraction for ancient writers and thinkers.

By A.D. 367, when Athanasius wrote one of his Festal Letters (episcopal greetings to other bishops at Easter), James had reached the 'top' class of Christian literature, and took its place with the other catholic letters in a list of recognized books. After that it is only the *order* of the books that varies. The list of books is not itself varied. Jerome, towards the end of the fourth century, reveals some doubt as to the origin of James. He says 'James who is called the brother of the Lord wrote one letter only, which itself is edited by another of the same name' (*Lives of Illustrious Men*, vol. II).

In comparatively modern times (A.D. 1530?) Luther referred to the letter as 'an epistle of straw'—'a right strawy epistle' to give a more vivid rendering of his German. This of course was because the letter seemed to contradict his very strong doctrine of 'justification by faith', which he had taken directly from Paul in Romans and Galatians.

CONCLUSIONS

What conclusions can be drawn from this collection of facts?
Not many with any degree of certainty. We can, however,
describe two different conclusions, both of which are held by
reputable scholars. In the last resort every student has to come
to his own opinion, in the light of the best knowledge that he
can command.

Let us first describe the 'traditional' or 'conservative' conclusion.

According to this view, James was written by the brother
of Jesus mentioned in Galatians. Because of the known date
of his death (approximately A.D. 62) the date of the letter must
be before then, but it *could* be written at almost any time
between the Crucifixion and that date. It would be natural
for it to be written towards the end of the available time, for
there was obviously a Greek-speaking Christian public to
write for. James's own excellent Greek has, on this view, to be
explained by the bilingual character of the Galilean population.
There must have been much Greek spoken in the Greek cities
of the Decapolis (around and east of the Sea of Galilee) but
how far ordinary Galileans spoke it we do not know. We
do know that the Gospels quote certain *Aramaic* sentences of
Jesus (e.g. *Talitha cum* = Get up, my child, Mark 5: 41) which
suggests that Aramaic was at least *his* normal language.

On this view, all the similarities to other New Testament
books have to be explained by saying that *either* the other
writers used James, *or* that all were drawing on a common
stock of tradition. The primitive nature of the teaching—its
practical, undogmatic character, with its elementary doctrine
about Jesus—fits in well with this view. Supporters of it would
say, 'the teaching is primitive because the book was primitive'.
Doctrine was simple, almost crude, because there had not been
time for it to become deep or subtle.

That is the old, traditional view, although it has to be supported today by arguments that were not necessary in the past.

At the opposite end of the scale is the 'advanced' or liberal view, which can be described as follows.

This book, it says, was unknown as Scripture as late as the end of the second century, although *The Shepherd of Hermas* (about A.D. 130) has several echoes of its wording. Had it really been written in the middle of the first century, it must surely have been accepted into the canon of Scripture before the middle of the *third* century, which is the earliest date we can give for its acceptance as part of the New Testament (Origen). This period was in fact a time when the so-called 'Catholic' or 'General' letters were winning their way slowly into the canon. James was a book which had to win its way.

On this view it is probable that the ascription at the beginning ('From James, a servant of God and the Lord Jesus Christ') is a typical 'apostolic' or 'semi-apostolic' label attached to a tract probably written about A.D. 100 or even later. It probably meant James 3, but it *could* have meant James 1. On the other hand, the book might really have been written by someone called James (it was a common name) but otherwise unknown to history.

This view explains the similarities to Matthew, 1 Peter, Romans and Galatians by the simple expedient of saying that the author of James knew these books, and alluded to them, either in agreement or in disagreement.

It may seem that the second view is easier to accept and leaves little to explain away. But it has to explain *something*. What it has to explain is how as late as A.D. 100 a book like James could still be written. Here is a tract, large parts of which might have been found in the Old Testament. References to Jesus are rare and almost casual. There is no hint of the Crucifixion, the Atonement, the Resurrection, or of the equal status of Jesus with God his Father. There *is* reference to the second coming (5: 7, and possibly 5: 9). There are no bishops or deacons, only elders (5: 14). The church gathering is still called a *synagogue* (the Greek word is disguised by the phrase 'place of worship' in the N.E.B. at 2: 2).

How do the exponents of the late, pseudonymous ('falsely labelled') view deal with all this? They have to say that somewhere, perhaps in a remote corner of Syria, there lurked a backward-looking group of Christians, Greek-speaking, but Hebrew-thinking, and that in such a community the outlook of James—simple, practical, opposed to ultra-clever, ultra-spiritual ideas—might and would survive. They would naturally associate their 'handbook' with a historic figure of the early days, and who better to choose than one of the Lord's family, who had represented the pro-Jewish element in the primitive church, and according to Acts was at the centre of the group which persuaded the great Paul of the Gentile mission to take a ritual vow rather than offend the strict Jews of Jerusalem.

Perhaps the writer of this commentary ought to say which view he thinks is most likely to represent the truth. He leans to the second view, not because it is free from difficulties, nor because the first view has any obviously fatal flaw in it. He does so for another reason. He thinks it would be a most extraordinary thing if while Jesus left no written works behind him, *two* of his brothers (for if James is accepted in this way the letter of Jude would have to be looked at as possibly a work by 'the brother of James') had written considerable tracts, in the Greek language, and that these had been preserved, had come into general use about two hundred years after they were written, and been treated as canonical ever since. When one knows the immense popularity in those times of attaching a new work to an old name (possibly because the old hero was thought to have inspired with his spirit a contemporary prophet) one cannot help hesitating long before accepting the traditional view. That the fellow-members of the carpenter's family at Nazareth *could* have left literary relics cannot be proved impossible. But is it really probable?

✻   ✻   ✻   ✻   ✻   ✻   ✻   ✻   ✻   ✻   ✻   ✻   ✻

Practical Religion

GREETING

1   FROM JAMES, a servant of God and the Lord Jesus
    Christ.

Greetings to the Twelve Tribes dispersed throughout
the world.

✳ The greeting follows the usual form in ancient letters,
'author's name...to (the recipients)'. Here the name of the
author is given as James, with only a very general description
of him: *a servant of God and the Lord Jesus Christ*. We have seen
(pp. 75–83, 93–5) the various persons who may be intended,
and the reasons for thinking that the word *James* here means
James the brother of Jesus. It is of course one thing to believe
that this is the James in question, and another to believe that he
was the actual author. We have seen that it was common to
attach famous names to tracts and books, and the history of the
early Church provides many examples of this. Different schools
of thought looked back to different apostles or other famous
leaders, and tended to claim their authority for what they
wanted to be read and believed. They may even have believed
that the ancient leaders *were* speaking through the lips or pen
of a contemporary prophet. Certainly of all the New Testament writings, this is the one that most closely fits in with the
conservative pro-Jewish attitude of 'James the Lord's brother',
though there is little in this letter about the precise commandments of the Jewish law.

Of other New Testament letters only one (Jude) begins with
the simple description *servant* (of God or Christ) for the author.
Romans begins 'From Paul, servant of Christ Jesus, apostle by
God's call'. It is very common, indeed almost regular, for
these opening greetings to contain a reference to God, usually

described as 'the Father' and to Jesus Christ although there are many different ways in which the two names are brought in. Here we have *a servant of God and the Lord Jesus Christ*.

In the early days of the Church Jesus Christ was often 'bracketed' with God in this way. It is an indirect testimony to the way in which they felt him to be closely linked with God, so closely in fact that he soon came to be actually called God, as seems to be the case in Titus 2: 13, 'the splendour of our great God and Saviour Christ Jesus'. Any difficulties about the author are repeated when we try to identify the recipients. These are said to be *the Twelve Tribes dispersed throughout the world*. The *Twelve Tribes* are of course the Hebrew nation, indeed the phrase is a synonym for that nation (see Matt. 19: 28). After the various exiles of the Jewish community only a small proportion of them lived in Palestine. They were to be found in Rome, Alexandria, the Greek cities, and away to the East. This non-Palestinian Judaism had a technical name 'the Dispersion' (Greek, *diaspora*). The N.E.B. disguises this technical title, and says *dispersed throughout the world*. The address shows that the document was not a letter in the sense of being actually sent to any particular person or persons. It was a tract, but it was felt to be suitable for Jews—indeed its message was not unlike the message addressed by Jesus to his contemporaries in his early teaching. (All this assumes that *Twelve Tribes* refers to the Jewish nation in the literal sense. The phrase could mean the new Israel = the Christian Church, but this is improbable.) *Greetings* translates the Greek word commonly used at the beginning of a letter. It happens to be used by James the Lord's brother in his letter after the Jerusalem conference, as is recorded in Acts 15: 23. *

THE WAY TO FORTITUDE AND WISDOM

My brothers, whenever you have to face trials of many 2
kinds, count yourselves supremely happy, in the know- 3
ledge that such testing of your faith breeds fortitude, and 4

if you give fortitude full play you will go on to complete
5 a balanced character that will fall short in nothing. If any
of you falls short in wisdom, he should ask God for it and
it will be given him, for God is a generous giver who
6 neither refuses nor reproaches anyone. But he must ask
in faith, without a doubt in his mind; for the doubter is
7 like a heaving sea ruffled by the wind. A man of that
8 kind must not expect the Lord to give him anything; he
is double-minded, and never can keep a steady course.

✳ The writer plunges at once into the moral and spiritual
teaching he has to give. There are no personal references, either
to his own circumstances or to those of his readers. It might
be thought that the reference to *trials of many kinds* (verse 2)
was a reference to particular troubles faced by his readers, but
this becomes less likely when we notice that I Peter has a very
similar passage almost at the beginning of that letter ('This
is cause for great joy, even though now you smart for a little
while, if need be, under trials of many kinds', I Pet. I: 6).
Both passages recall Matt. 5: II, I2, 'How blest you are, when
you suffer insults and persecution and every kind of calumny
for my sake. Accept it with gladness.…'
    The idea that trouble may be used by God to bring blessing
to the sufferer is not unknown in the Old Testament (see,
e.g. Ps. II9: 7I, 'It is good for me that I have been afflicted;
that I might learn thy statutes', and the whole story of Job's
troubles as told in the book of Job), but the idea of actually re-
joicing in suffering is a New Testament thought. Bacon's
remark is mostly justified: 'Prosperity is the blessing of the
Old Testament, adversity the blessing of the New.' Here the
joyful acceptance of suffering is said to lead to *fortitude* (verses 3,
4). This is the N.E.B. translation of the Greek word for endurance, 'sticking it out'. Paul has almost the same thought
in Rom. 5: 3, 4: 'let us even exult in our present sufferings,
because we know that suffering trains us to endure, and en-

durance brings proof that we have stood the test...'. *A balanced character that will fall short in nothing* (verse 4) is a free translation—'perfect and complete, not lacking in anything' is a more literal translation. *Balanced character* suggests *either* the point of view of the modern psychologist, *or* of Greek philosophers like Aristotle, with his idea of the golden mean. Neither is quite what we should look for in James.

The second half of the paragraph calls on the readers to seek wisdom from God if they know they need it. He, the writer says, *is a generous giver*. But the petitioner must *ask in faith, without a doubt in his mind* (verse 6). Doubt means double-mindedness (verse 8) and leads to a course as unstable as a ruffled sea (verse 6).

Here are reminiscences of the famous Old Testament example of wisdom, Solomon. In I Kings 3: 7–14, we read the story of how Solomon, as a young king, asked from God the gift of wisdom and how God gave him 'a wise and understanding heart'. This is told as part of a dream, but the picture became an accepted part of the Hebrew tradition—Solomon was wise, the story went, because God heard his prayer. The 'wisdom' literature of the Old Testament and Apocrypha is mostly linked with Solomon's name (e.g. The Proverbs of Solomon, The Wisdom of Solomon). The promise of *wisdom* in James is given in words which recall words of Jesus in the Gospels, e.g. Matt. 7: 7, 8, 'Ask, and you will receive; seek, and you will find; knock, and the door will be opened. For everyone who asks receives...'.

The figure of the *heaving sea* is the first of a number of vivid illustrations from nature in this letter. Several of them are connected with water. See, besides this one, 3: 4, 5 (ships and their rudders), 3: 11, 12 ('fresh and brackish water'), 5: 7, 8 and 16–18 (rain and the crops).

The necessity of faith as a condition for the obtaining of petitions (getting 'answers to prayer') is repeatedly stressed in the Gospels, especially in Mark 11: 22–4, a passage which has great similarity with James I: 5–8. Many have deduced from

passages of this sort that a firm belief that certain blessings will
be given in answer to prayer, itself guarantees the granting of
the boon. Experience shows that this view is altogether too
naïve. Many confident prayers for the recovery of sick people,
or the protection of those in danger, have not been 'answered'
in the way the petitioner hoped for. On the other side, the
words of Heb. 11: 6 represent a necessary element in all prayer:
'anyone who comes to God must believe that he exists and
that he rewards those who search for him'. Faith in God's
reality, power and love releases energy in the spiritual world
—this is quite different from thinking that 'so much certainty'
guarantees 'so much result' in the material world. *

POVERTY AND WEALTH

9 The brother in humble circumstances may well be proud
10 that God lifts him up; and the wealthy brother must find
his pride in being brought low. For the rich man will
11 disappear like the flower of the field; once the sun is up
with its scorching heat the flower withers, its petals fall,
and what was lovely to look at is lost for ever. So shall
the rich man wither away as he goes about his business.

* One of the recurrent themes in James is the contrast between the rich and the poor. The rich are shown up in a bad
light. Their present behaviour is criticized ('are not the rich
your oppressors?', 2: 6) and their prospects are said to be
poor. In these verses (1: 9, 10) *the brother in humble circumstances* is encouraged to boast of, to be proud of the fact that
God lifts him up—in the Greek the subject of the boasting is
just 'his elevation'. Two Greek words are being thrown into
contrast here, *tapeinos*, humble, lowly, and *hupsos*, elevation,
being uplifted. These two words, or the verbs made up from
them, are often contrasted in the New Testament. See, e.g.
Matt. 23: 12, 'For whoever exalts himself will be humbled;
and whoever humbles himself will be exalted'. A rather

different thought, but making use of the same words, is found in 2 Cor. 11: 7, 'Or was this my offence, that I made no charge for preaching the gospel of God, lowering myself to help in raising you?' In James *humble* is contrasted with *wealthy*, thus interpreting the sequence *humble* and 'exalted' in terms of financial and social position. There is no great difficulty in advising *the brother in humble circumstances* to rejoice in the fact that he is, or will be, lifted up. This point is made in 1 Pet. 5: 6, 'Humble yourselves then under God's mighty hand, and he will lift you up in due time'. It is harder to see what is meant when *the wealthy brother* is told to be proud of being brought low. This could mean that the rejection of wealth as a source of pride and prestige brought its bearer back to the *privileged* position of the poor (cf. Luke 6: 20, 'How blest are you who are poor; the kingdom of God is yours') or it might mean that he really must be brought low. The future of the rich man in any case is painted in sombre colours. His glory will be as shortlived as that of a lovely flower in a scorching hot sun. These lines about the flower are borrowed from Isa. 40: 6, 7, as also in 1 Pet. 1: 24, another strong suggestion that there is some connexion between 1 Peter and James. *

WHERE TEMPTATION COMES FROM

Happy the man who remains steadfast under trial, for 12 having passed that test he will receive for his prize the gift of life promised to those who love God. No one under 13 trial or temptation should say, 'I am being tempted by God'; for God is untouched by evil, and does not himself tempt anyone. Temptation arises when a man is enticed 14 and lured away by his own lust; then lust conceives, and 15 gives birth to sin; and sin full-grown breeds death.

* This paragraph begins with a repetition of the points made in 1: 2 about the value of being tested under trials, in order to

bring out fortitude and faith. Here, however, the hoped-for result is not so much a character tried and found reliable, but *the gift of life promised to those who love God* (verse 12). The Greek has 'the crown of life', the crown, that is, that consists of life. The metaphor is taken from the world of athletic contest, where the victor was given a crown, or of courtly life and dignity. Cf. Rev. 2: 10, 'Only be faithful till death, and I will give you the crown of life'. *Those who love God* are singled out for special rewards in various scriptural passages, notably in 1 Cor. 2: 9, 'Things beyond our imagining, all prepared by God for those who love him'.

In the remaining verses of this paragraph, the readers are warned not to attribute their temptations to God. Perhaps some had misunderstood the Lord's Prayer, 'Lead us not into temptation', and deduced from this phrase the idea that God might really tempt his people. No, says our writer. God is untempted and untemptable (the Greek word covers a wide range of meaning) and therefore he does not tempt. *Temptation arises*, says James, *when a man is enticed and lured away by his own lust*. Like Jesus, the author sees the inner heart of man as the source of evil (cf. Mark 7: 21–3, 'For from inside, out of a man's heart, come evil thoughts, acts of fornication, of theft, murder, adultery. . . these evil things all come from inside, and they defile the man'). All this does not mean that God has not done his work as Creator well: it means that man has allowed good things in his make-up to get out of proportion, out of hand, distorted and perverted. *Lust* (verse 14) is an old English word that originally meant just *desire* ('What man is he that lusteth to live?' Ps. 34: 12 in the Book of Common Prayer—what man is there that wants to live?) but it has come to mean 'desire gone wrong', 'desire allowed to take control', and hence exactly translates the Greek word used here. The paragraph ends with a sequence of pictures suitably attached to the word 'lust': *lust conceives, and gives birth to sin. Sin full-grown breeds death*. The idea that death was in some way the result of sin was part of the traditional belief of the Jews. It goes back to Gen. 2: 17, 'of the tree of the knowledge of good and evil, thou shalt not eat of it: for in the day that thou eatest thereof thou shalt surely die'. It is alluded to in Rom. 5: 12, 'It was through one man that sin entered the world, and through sin death, and thus death pervaded the whole human race...', and in Rom. 6: 23, 'For sin pays a wage, and the wage is death'. In the literal, physical sense it is almost impossible to believe this, for death is common to all living creatures. Were it not for death, the world could not sustain any species of life. But there was a true insight in the old belief, namely that true life was life lived in fellowship with God, and was hence indestructible. Of such life sin was the enemy, and thus 'death and sin' were the two supreme enemies of human hope and happiness. ✷

GOD THE SOURCE OF ALL GOOD

Do not deceive yourselves, my friends. All good giving 16,17 and every perfect gift comes from above, from the Father of the lights of heaven. With him there is no variation, no play of passing shadows. Of his set purpose, by declaring 18 the truth, he gave us birth to be a kind of firstfruits of his creatures.

✷ The thought that God could be the source of temptation being thus rejected, the writer shows that on the contrary it is the good things that come from him. *All good giving and every perfect gift comes from above* (verse 17). There is a contrast in the Greek between the word translated *giving* (*dosis*) and that translated *gift* (*dōrēma*). The one emphasizes the action; the other the object or result of the action, the gift. Both come (the N.E.B. is surely careless in English grammar in saying *comes!*) from above. They come down *from the Father of the lights of heaven* (verse 17). The N.E.B. takes *lights* in the sense of stars, probably rightly, but the idea that God is light was common enough as, e.g. in 1 John 1: 5, 'God is light, and in him there is no darkness at all'. *With him*, we read (verse 17) *there is no variation, no play of passing shadows*. It is tempting to think that the writer, having once got into an astronomical atmosphere, with *Father of the lights of heaven*, carried on with figures of speech from that branch of knowledge. Then he would have meant 'with God there is no continual change'. The Greek word for variation is *parallagē*, which will remind students of optics of the English word 'parallax'—this means the variation in appearance when two or more objects are looked at from different points—sometimes they are 'in line', sometimes clearly separated. 'With God', he might have continued, 'there is no overshadowing of his light, such as the moon undergoes as it turns in the heaven.' Probably, however, he was not thinking in scientific terms at all, but just using language from his wide vocabulary to suggest variation and changefulness. These, he says, are absent from God, who is permanently and perfectly good. *Play of passing shadows* is an attractive rendering, if a very free one, of the Greek 'overshadowing of the turn'.

The last sentence of the paragraph, *Of his set purpose, by declaring the truth, he gave us birth to be a kind of firstfruits of his creatures* (verse 18), does not cling very closely to the previous or to the following words. The writer probably wanted to say that God's supreme gift to men—adoption into his family, new birth through the Gospel—was no accident. God had given this gift *of...set purpose*. It was characteristic of the unlimited and unalterable goodness of the Divine Giver. The idea of Christians being 'born', or 'begotten' (the N.E.B has not been able to find a modern equivalent for the old-fashioned word) through the Gospel is not uncommon in the New Testament. See especially a passage very similar to this in 1 Pet. 1: 23, 'You have been born anew, not of mortal parentage but of immortal, through the living and enduring word of God'. *A kind of firstfruits of his creatures* (verse 18) is a figure of speech taken from the Old Testament (e.g. Deut. 18: 4, 'The firstfruits of thy corn, of thy wine and of thine oil, and the first of the fleece of thy sheep, shalt thou give him'). The earliest produce of the year was offered to God, as a sign that all belonged to him. So the writer says that the Christians had been 'brought to birth' as the first product of the spread of the Gospel. So Paul in Rom. 16: 5 speaks of 'Epaenetus, the first convert to Christ in Asia', literally, 'the firstfruits of Asia'. ✳

MORAL RESULTS FROM HEARING THE GOSPEL

Of that you may be certain, my friends. But each of you 19 must be quick to listen, slow to speak, and slow to be angry. For a man's anger cannot promote the justice of 20 God. Away then with all that is sordid, and the malice 21 that hurries to excess, and quietly accept the message planted in your hearts, which can bring you salvation.

✳ This paragraph begins and ends with the idea of *listening—each of you must be quick to listen* (verse 19), *quietly accept the message planted in your hearts* (verse 21). These phrases could follow on naturally the thought of the Gospel coming to the ears and hearts of men with saving power as in verse 18. But in between, the listening is interpreted in the ordinary sense, especially in the sense of controlling the tongue, avoiding hasty, angry words. *Man's anger cannot promote the justice of God* (verse 20). Justice is the translation of *dikaiosunē*, a famous New Testament word, which appears in older versions as 'righteousness': 'justice' gives its meaning much more clearly to the modern world. Then comes the thought that certain things are incompatible with the new relationship set up between the new-born, or newly adopted children of God and their Father. In all the New Testament instructional passages there are rules as to things that must be parted with (e.g. Eph. 4: 28, 'the thief must give up stealing'; Eph. 4: 25, 'then throw off falsehood'). Here the alien elements are described as *all that is sordid* and *the malice that hurries to excess* (verse 21). The Greek does not actually suggest 'hurrying to excess', but rather the 'overflowing', or 'effervescence of malice'. As Jesus says in Matt. 12: 34, 'the words that the mouth utters come from the overflowing of the heart'. ✶

HEARING THE MESSAGE IS NOT ENOUGH

22 Only be sure that you act on the message and do not merely listen; for that would be to mislead yourselves.
23 A man who listens to the message but never acts upon it is like one who looks in a mirror at the face nature gave him.
24 He glances at himself and goes away, and at once forgets
25 what he looked like. But the man who looks closely into the perfect law, the law that makes us free, and who lives in its company, does not forget what he hears, but acts upon it; and that is the man who by acting will find happiness.

✶ This letter is severely practical in tone. The writer has just referred to *the message...which can bring you salvation* (verse 21) and now hastens to point out that hearing this message is not all that is required: *only be sure that you act on the message and do not merely listen* (verse 22). Here the writer is close to the recorded teaching of Jesus. In Matt. 7: 24–7 the Sermon on the Mount ends with the parable of the two men, one of whom built his house on rock and the other on sand. The former was the man who heard the words of Jesus and acted on them; the latter, one who heard them and did not act on them.

The idea behind the parable of the sower (Mark 4: 4–20) though not identical, is very similar. The writer of James uses a strange, apparently far-fetched figure of speech to illustrate his point. He says that the *man who listens to the message but never acts upon it is* like a man who takes a brief glance in a mirror, sees himself, and then forgets all about what he saw. *The face nature gave him* is a bold effort to make sense of a strange expression in the Greek. James speaks of a man considering 'the face of his birth', his *genesis* (the actual Greek

word used) or his origin. This word occurs again at 3: 6 when
it is translated 'existence'. The word seems to begin by
meaning 'birth' but is extended to apply to the whole of life.
The kind of mirror commonly used was a circular disk of
burnished copper or similar material. It is useless to press the
analogy too far. All that is meant is that the momentary
glance at the mirror corresponds to the very short-lived attention the 'non-doer' devotes to the message he hears. Then, as
so often, the writer takes up one idea in one sentence, and
develops it in quite a different direction. He thinks of another
kind of look—a close look—directed not to the mirror, but
to *the perfect law, the law that makes us free* (verse 25). What does
he mean by that? He helps us a little by using the phrase
again at 2: 12, where he says that Christians are to be judged
'under a law of freedom'. What he is meaning is that the
Christians, like the pre-Christian Jews, have a law to guide
them. The law is probably the teaching of Jesus, and he calls
this 'a law of freedom' to distinguish it from the Jewish law,
which according to Christian leaders like Paul produced an
oppressive sense of bondage (e.g. Gal. 4: 25, 'Jerusalem of
today...her children are in slavery', and Rom. 8: 2, 'in
Christ Jesus the life-giving law of the Spirit has set you free
from the law of sin and death'). *

RELIGION—FALSE AND TRUE

A man may think he is religious, but if he has no control 26
over his tongue, he is deceiving himself; that man's religion is futile. The kind of religion which is without stain 27
or fault in the sight of God our Father is this: to go to the
help of orphans and widows in their distress and keep
oneself untarnished by the world.

* In verse 26 the writer states one of his great principles, to
which he will return in 3: 1–12. The principle is that in good
Christian living the control of the tongue—what you say—

is of special importance. It is difficult not to feel that he has got this matter somewhat out of proportion. It is not only the tongue that needs control, but also the hand, the expression on the face, the appetite, the sexual nature. But words are of great importance, for words are the chief means whereby one personality communicates with another. Anyway, his point is plain enough, and everyone has to come to terms with it: a wild and unruly tongue reveals a fundamental fault in character. The only religion compatible with it is a religion which is clearly *futile* (verse 26). But immediately he feels the need to describe *the kind of religion* (verse 27) that is *not* futile, a kind which is faultless *in the sight of God our Father* (there is no Greek word in the text corresponding to 'our', but the Greek says 'God and Father' in such a way as almost to suggest 'our Father, God' as a translation). The pure religion that is acceptable with God is marked by practical kindness—going *to the help of orphans and widows in their distress* (verse 27)— and personal purity—keeping *oneself untarnished by the world* (verse 27). The first of these two features is in line with the prophets' teaching that the unprotected members of the community are a special responsibility to those who wish to obey God's commands. In this book *the world* is used much as it is in the Johannine letters (e.g. 1 John 2: 15, 'Anyone who loves the world is a stranger to the Father's love'). It means human society in so far as it is alien to God's will and purpose. The importance of practical service to the helpless echoes the importance given to it by Jesus, e.g. in the parable of the sheep and the goats (Matt. 25: 31–46). ✳

THE SIN OF SNOBBERY

2 My brothers, believing as you do in our Lord Jesus Christ,
2 who reigns in glory, you must never show snobbery. For instance, two visitors may enter your place of worship, one a well-dressed man with gold rings, and the other a

poor man in shabby clothes. Suppose you pay special 3
attention to the well-dressed man and say to him, 'Please
take this seat', while to the poor man you say, 'You can
stand; or you may sit here on the floor by my footstool',
do you not see that you are inconsistent and judge by 4
false standards?

Listen, my friends. Has not God chosen those who are 5
poor in the eyes of the world to be rich in faith and to
inherit the kingdom he has promised to those who love
him? And yet you have insulted the poor man. More- 6
over, are not the rich your oppressors? Is it not they who
drag you into court and pour contempt on the honoured 7
name by which God has claimed you?

٭ The first of the two paragraphs included in this section condemns snobbery, particularly in the assembly of the Church.
Notice first of all the reference to the readers' Christian faith:
believing as you do in our Lord Jesus Christ, who reigns in glory
(verse 1). This is one of the very few explicit references to
Jesus in the letter. The only other certain one is in 1: 1, but
several of the references to 'the Lord' probably mean Jesus
rather than God the Father, especially two verses (5: 7 and 8)
referring to 'the coming of the Lord'. Notice also the simple
form of the belief: it consists in believing in Jesus as the one
who *reigns in glory*. In primitive times the core of the faith was
to believe that Jesus was risen, exalted, at the right hand of God
(cf. 1 Cor. 12: 3, 'no one can say "Jesus is Lord!" except
under the influence of the Holy Spirit'). Here the point is
that Jesus who taught service and self-sacrifice is now 'in
power', and hence anything like snobbery offends against his
will and purpose. Snobbery is a good modern word for the
Greek word used in verse 1, and it fits this context well. The
root meaning, however, is not quite 'snobbery' but something
more like 'favouritism', or 'discrimination'.

The next few verses (2–4) describe a possible scene in a place of meeting. *Your place of worship* (verse 2) is literally, in the Greek, 'your synagogue'. This use of words has been thought to suggest *either* that this passage has been borrowed from some Jewish tract or sermon *or* that the whole of James is basically Jewish, with some Christian adaptations *or* that this Christian community had not yet separated from the Jewish synagogue, *or* was still close enough to it to use its phraseology. The N.E.B. treats it as a general word—'gathering-place'— and then paraphrases to 'place of worship', thereby concealing a real, but almost insoluble problem of interpretation. The passage certainly suggests a very highly organized meeting with good seats and bad seats, and at least some wealthy attenders (*a well-dressed man with gold rings*, verse 2). It has to be admitted that the Church in later ages has not always obeyed James's instruction in these matters. Eighteenth- and nineteenth-century English churches often had an elaborate pew for the principal family. Poorer worshippers were kept in obscure corners of the church, and to this day it is sometimes hard to get 'village' people to sit in the front half of a country church. *You...judge by false standards* (verse 4) is a smooth translation of a difficult Greek phrase which probably means 'you have become judges inspired by evil considerations'.

Then, in the second paragraph, (verses 5–7) the writer goes on to a general attack on the rich and an exaltation of the poor. It had long been a traditional Jewish belief that 'the poor in the land' were specially the subject of God's care and approval. This did not prevent the Sadducees and Pharisees teaching that wealth showed, or made possible, God's blessing. Jesus took up the classical 'pro-poor' attitude (see especially Luke 6: 20, 'How blest are you who are poor; the kingdom of God is yours', which is probably closer to the original form of the saying than that in Matt. 5: 3, 'How blest are those who know that they are poor [lit. the poor in spirit]; the kingdom of Heaven is theirs'). James has in mind for commendation *those who are poor in the eyes of the world*. These are *to be rich*

*in faith and to inherit the kingdom he has promised to those who
love him* (verse 5). On this last phrase see commentary on 1:
12. Verses 6 and 7 assume that in general *the rich* are hostile,
though the passage suggests that at least an occasional rich
man appeared at the 'church service'. The rich are taken to
represent the persecuting element—they drag the poor into
court and pour contempt *on the honoured name* by which God
has claimed them (verse 7). *Honoured name*: the Dead Sea
Scrolls (*Manual of Discipline*, 6: 27) have this phrase: 'the
name honoured above all...names'. Literally this text reads
'do they not blaspheme the noble name which was called over
you', presumably meaning that the oppressors mocked the
Christians 'because of the name' (cf. 1 Pet. 4: 16), i.e. they
had taken Christ's name on themselves at baptism, and this
was a source of obloquy and ridicule in the courts. *

THE LAW OF LOVE

If, however, you are observing the sovereign law laid 8
down in Scripture, 'Love your neighbour as yourself',
that is excellent. But if you show snobbery, you are 9
committing a sin and you stand convicted by that law as
transgressors. For if a man keeps the whole law apart 10
from one single point, he is guilty of breaking all of it.
For the One who said, 'Thou shalt not commit adultery', 11
said also, 'Thou shalt not commit murder.' You may
not be an adulterer, but if you commit murder you are a
law-breaker all the same. Always speak and act as men 12
who are to be judged under a law of freedom. In that 13
judgement there will be no mercy for the man who has
shown no mercy. Mercy triumphs over judgement.

* This paragraph picks up the thought of verse 4, there having
been a slight interruption of the argument in verses 5–7. The
sovereign law (verse 8)—compare *perfect law* (1: 25) and *law of*

freedom (verse 12)—is the law as summed up by Jesus, *Love your neighbour as yourself* (verse 8, see also Matt. 22: 39, where Jesus uses these words to sum up that part of God's law which concerns other people). Our writer says that *snobbery* (verse 9) is an offence against this law of love. Then he stresses that all the commandments (he quotes the sixth and seventh of the Ten Commandments) are given by the same lawgiver. An offence in one point therefore carries the same consequences of a broken personal relationship as an offence in all. Verses 12 and 13 contain much thought in a very few words. What the writer means to say is this: 'Christians must not think they are free from all the constraints of law. They are not. Their law, however, is not a law that makes them slaves. It is a law of love, and this law is a law characterized by freedom and responsibility.' As Jesus had taught, mercy will be shown to those who themselves have shown mercy. (Compare Matt. 5: 7, 'How blest are those who show mercy; mercy shall be shown to them'.) *Mercy triumphs over judgement* (verse 13). Mercy has the last word.

The passage from verse 8 to verse 11 has some similarity to Paul's words in Rom. 13: 8, 9, 'He who loves his neighbour has satisfied every claim of the law. For the commandments, "Thou shalt not commit adultery, thou shalt not kill, thou shalt not steal, thou shalt not covet", and any other commandment there may be, are all summed up in the one rule, "Love your neighbour as yourself"'. The similarity is important in connexion with the next section of James (2: 14–26) where it is an open question whether this passage is itself a reply to Pauline passages on faith and works, or whether, as some think, Paul himself was replying to James. *

FAITH WITHOUT DEEDS IS USELESS

14 My brothers, what use is it for a man to say he has faith when he does nothing to show it? Can that faith save
15 him? Suppose a brother or a sister is in rags with not

enough food for the day, and one of you says, 'Good 16
luck to you, keep yourselves warm, and have plenty to
eat', but does nothing to supply their bodily needs, what
is the good of that? So with faith; if it does not lead to 17
action, it is in itself a lifeless thing.

But someone may object: 'Here is one who claims to 18
have faith and another who points to his deeds.' To which
I reply: 'Prove to me that this faith you speak of is real
though not accompanied by deeds, and by my deeds I
will prove to you my faith.' You have faith enough to 19
believe that there is one God. Excellent! The devils have
faith like that, and it makes them tremble. But can you 20
not see, you quibbler, that faith divorced from deeds is
barren? Was it not by his action, in offering his son Isaac 21
upon the altar, that our father Abraham was justified?
Surely you can see that faith was at work in his actions, 22
and that by these actions the integrity of his faith was fully
proved. Here was fulfilment of the words of Scripture: 23
'Abraham put his faith in God, and that faith was counted
to him as righteousness'; and elsewhere he is called 'God's
friend'. You see then that a man is justified by deeds and 24
not by faith in itself. The same is true of the prostitute 25
Rahab also. Was not she justified by her action in welcoming the messengers into her house and sending them away
by a different route? As the body is dead when there is 26
no breath left in it, so faith divorced from deeds is lifeless
as a corpse.

✻ The passage here chosen for comment is longer than most
selected in this commentary, but it cannot really be broken up.
It is a continuous passage, dealing with the one subject, the
relation between faith and action in the Christian religion.

Before we examine it in detail, it is necessary to recall that
a prominent viewpoint in Paul's writings is the importance of
faith and faith alone in the process whereby men are 'justified',
put right with God. The important passages (though not the
only ones) are Gal. 2: 15, 16, and Rom. 3: 19–28. One must
also include the whole of Rom. 4 where there is a prolonged
argument attempting to prove that Abraham was put right
with God by his faith, quite apart from his deeds. Paul's
position, to sum it up in broad terms was this: Jews had had
God's *law* for centuries but people just could not keep it. It only
made them conscious of their sins, and far from giving them
life and joy, it produced misery and death. Instead, men should
pin their faith on Christ crucified and risen, One who had
obeyed God perfectly. If, giving up all their own efforts, they
would look to him, they would be saved by grace, through
faith. This is what is meant by the doctrine which became the
foundation-stone of the Reformation, justification by faith.

It does not follow from this—as unfortunately many have
thought, the writer of James possibly being among them—
that Paul was indifferent to the practical behaviour of his converts. He strongly repudiated the idea that those who were
freed from sin should continue in a life of sin. 'What then?
Are we to sin because we are not under law but under grace?
Of course not' (Rom. 6: 15). He believed that faith should
and could 'work' by love.

Now come back to Jas. 2: 14–26. Verses 14–17 lay down the
thesis that faith unaccompanied by a good life is useless. *My
brothers, what use is it for a man to say he has faith when he does
nothing to show it?* (verse 14). It is as useless, he says, as if
someone said to a ragged, hungry beggar 'keep yourself warm
and have plenty to eat' (verse 16) without giving him clothes
or food. Here the point is almost identical with that made in
1 John 3: 17, 'But if a man has enough to live on, and yet when
he sees his brother in need shuts up his heart against him, how
can it be said that divine love dwells in him?' It would seem
that professions of faith, and claims to a life in fellowship with

God in Christ were common, and that they were not always accompanied with those practical signs of Christian character which should have accompanied faith.

James comes out strongly against the view that faith *can* exist without deeds. To begin with, the point is made that faith without deeds cannot be seen or proved to exist. That is the point of the curious section (verse 18) giving the views of an unidentified 'objector'. The N.E.B. has smoothed away the basic difficulties of this passage, and it will be best first to explain the text as presented in the N.E.B.

The writer has made his point in verse 17 that faith without action is lifeless. Then he contemplates an objector getting up and saying, 'Wait a minute! Isn't it possible for one man to be distinguished for his faith and another for his deeds?' (paraphrasing verse 18, first part). This is meant to be an argument *against* the view of James that faith and deeds must be inextricably linked together. So James replies, 'No! how can a man show faith apart from works to accord with it? It is only by deeds that faith can be shown to exist in reality'. (This is a paraphrase of the second part of verse 18.)

This is all very well, and is possibly what the writer of James meant. It must be said, however, that it is not the only, perhaps not the most natural, way of taking the Greek. The words in the N.E.B. *To which I reply* (middle of verse 18) are not in the Greek at all. They make a distinction of speaker between the *objector's* words and the words beginning, *Prove to me that this faith*, etc. There is nothing in the Greek to make it clear that a change of speaker is intended. If, however, a change is *not* intended we are left with the curious position that the objector appears to be putting the same point of view as the writer of James. The words *But someone may object* would be better out of the way, but of course they cannot be got rid of. This is all so difficult that some early manuscripts have reversed the order of *faith* and *deeds* in the first part of verse 18. This is mentioned only to show that in the early centuries the difficulties we notice were well understood.

In verse 19 the inadequacy of mere intellectual belief is pointed out. The objector is granted his point—he believes that there is one God (virtually this means the Jewish faith in monotheism, though the classic creed of Judaism was to believe in one *Lord*, i.e. God *in* his sovereignty over, and care for his people, cf. Deut. 6: 4). But, James goes on, devils may believe in this sense, and far from this giving them life and peace, it makes them tremble for fear.

In verse 20 the writer returns to his main point, that faith is *barren* when *divorced from deeds*. He now refers to the famous case of Abraham. He says that it was by his obedience *in offering his son Isaac upon the altar* that he was *justified* (verse 21). Against this background he quotes the well-known verse, Gen. 15: 6, 'Abraham put his faith in God, and that faith was counted to him as righteousness', to quote the words in the N.E.B. version of James. (Actually the N.E.B. goes further than the Greek in the second part of the verse. The Greek just says 'Abraham believed in God, and it was reckoned to him for righteousness'.) Now the interesting thing is that Paul quotes this same verse in Rom. 4: 3, but uses it to prove that Abraham was justified by his *faith* not by his *deeds*. It is this that has led many to think that *either* Paul is correcting James or James is correcting Paul. But neither deduction is necessary. The manner of Abraham's justification was already the subject of argument among Jewish scholars before Paul or James. Even in 1 Macc. 2: 52 the point had been raised; 'Was not Abraham found faithful in temptation, and it was reckoned unto him for righteousness?' In addition to this view, namely that Abraham was counted righteous because he sacrificed Isaac, some held that he obtained this status by believing God's promise about descendants (Gen. 15: 6) or by obeying the law by anticipation (Jubilees 15: 1 ff.).

The case of Rahab is raised in verse 24. Her story is found in Josh. 2: 4 ff. She had little to commend her as far as her way of life was concerned (she was a prostitute). But in a dim way she discerned God's purpose for his people, and co-operated with it. So she became an example of faith, and is quoted as such in Heb. 11: 31 (not Pauline, and therefore no evidence, one way or the other, for a literary connexion between Paul and James).

Actually the gap between Paul and James is much smaller than a superficial comparison of their words would suggest. Paul insists that justification is by faith, not by works, though he clearly expects faith to bear fruit in love. James cries down faith without deeds, but makes it clear that the faith he cries down is a barren intellectual assent not a vital commitment of the whole personality to God in Christ. It is this living and obedient trust that carries with it the promises made so often in the Bible to 'them *that believe*'. ✶

THE FAR-REACHING EFFECTS OF WHAT WE SAY

My brothers, not many of you should become teachers, **3** for you may be certain that we who teach shall ourselves be judged with greater strictness. All of us often go 2 wrong; the man who never says a wrong thing is a perfect character, able to bridle his whole being. If we put bits 3 into horses' mouths to make them obey our will, we can direct their whole body. Or think of ships: large they 4 may be, yet even when driven by strong gales they can be directed by a tiny rudder on whatever course the helmsman chooses. So with the tongue. It is a small member 5 but it can make huge claims.

✶ In this chapter James embarks upon one of his main themes, that of the great importance of the things we say, or as he would put it, of the tongue. The writer arrives at this theme almost accidentally. He says in verse 1 that it is better for *not many* of them to *become teachers*, because those *who teach* will be judged *with greater strictness*. Teachers were a recognized group in the primitive church, though possibly they 'over-lapped' with other groups. In Eph. 4: 11 they are bracketed with 'pastors'—'some pastors and teachers'—following on in the series 'apostles, prophets, evangelists'. In Acts 13: 1 they are bracketed with prophets—'There were...certain prophets and teachers'. In 1 Tim. 3: 2 it is said that the bishop must be 'a good teacher'. Teaching probably meant teaching those who were preparing for baptism, and other new converts. Among the subjects to be taught were the outlines of the teaching and life of Jesus (the Gospels possibly were written as handbooks for this purpose) and the evidence provided by the Old Testament that Jesus measured up to what was expected of 'the Christ'. That a special responsibility rests on those who take on the task of teaching others is suggested by common sense and daily experience as well as hints in the Bible (see e.g. Titus 2: 8). *All of us often go wrong* (verse 2), literally, 'all of us stumble in many ways'. But, the writer says, or implies, the easiest sin of all is a sin of speech—*the man who never says a wrong thing is a perfect character* (verse 2). This is rather an extreme way of putting something which is certainly true, namely that a man with perfect control of his tongue would certainly be a man of outstanding quality and character. He might not actually be *perfect*, but he would certainly be 'mature' which is another meaning of the Greek word (*teleios*). He would be *able to bridle his whole being* (verse 2). This is the cue which leads the writer on to one of his most well-known passages in which he develops the theme of 'small things with big consequences'. His first illustration is the bit in the horses' mouths (verse 3). The small iron object, if put in the horse's mouth, can be used to lead or guide the whole great animal. Then the writer thinks of ships; *large they may be, yet even when driven by strong gales they can be directed by a tiny rudder* (verse 4). The 'slight push' of the helmsman's hand on the tiller governs the course of the great ship. So, we read, it is with the tongue. It is *a small member* (verse 5) *but it can* (rightly) *make huge claims.*

The vivid illustrations from horsemanship and sailing are characteristic of James. We are no longer in the atmosphere of peasant Galilee, but in one which includes these activities of the wider world. The word for rudder is in Greek *pedalion* (cf. pedal in a car, 'brake-pedal', etc.). ✳

THE UNLIMITED CONSEQUENCES OF
UNCONTROLLED SPEECH

What a huge stack of timber can be set ablaze by the tiniest spark! And the tongue is in effect a fire. It repre- 6 sents among our members the world with all its wicked- ness; it pollutes our whole being; it keeps the wheel of our existence red-hot, and its flames are fed by hell. Beasts 7 and birds of every kind, creatures that crawl on the ground or swim in the sea, can be subdued and have been subdued by mankind; but no man can subdue the tongue. It is an 8 intractable evil, charged with deadly venom. We use it 9 to sing the praises of our Lord and Father, and we use it to invoke curses upon our fellow-men who are made in God's likeness. Out of the same mouth come praises and 10 curses. My brothers, this should not be so. Does a foun- 11 tain gush with both fresh and brackish water from the same opening? Can a fig-tree, my brothers, yield olives, 12 or a vine figs? No more does salt water yield fresh.

✳ Now another metaphor comes to the writer's mind—that of fire. *What a huge stack of timber can be set ablaze by the tiniest spark* (verse 5). This translation, though attractive for its English style, hardly suggests the crisp, terse Greek. 'What a blaze from what a spark' suggests the style of the original, an example of that highly compressed use of the Greek language which many feel could hardly be natural to a carpenter's son from Nazareth. The 'spark–blaze' contrast was

in line with the 'bit–horse', 'rudder–ship' sequence of contrasts, but having once said *fire* the writer forgets about the
'spark–blaze' idea and goes on to say (verse 6) *And the tongue
is…a fire*. From *And the tongue* to *pollutes our whole being*
there is a clear enough line of thought in the N.E.B. It is not
so clear in the original Greek; indeed the sentence can be
punctuated in a number of ways, each of which leads to a
different translation. There are isolated phrases in the Greek
such as 'the tongue [is a] fire', and 'the world of wickedness'.
Some have thought that these were originally paragraph
headings, later accidentally incorporated into the text. If this
were so, the translation would be a good deal easier. But the
general meaning is fairly clear. *The tongue*, we read, *is…a fire*.
It sets things going, and once they are set going, cannot stop
them again. *Among our members*, our organs (verse 6), it consti-
tutes, or *represents…the world with all its wickedness*. It *pollutes
our whole being*. Then comes a cryptic phrase, skilfully turned
into English in the N.E.B.: *it keeps the wheel of our existence
red-hot* (verse 6). The figure seems to be that of a chariot-
wheel set on fire by its axle which has developed too much
friction. The meaning would be 'just as an axle sets a wheel
on fire, so the tongue sets our whole existence on fire'. The
Greek behind *wheel of our existence* could, however, mean 'the
course of our life' or 'the whole round of our existence' (birth
to death). It is impossible to be absolutely sure, as even the
same word in Greek (*trochos*) can mean two different things—
wheel or course—according to the position of the accent,
which does not appear at all in the manuscripts written entirely
in Greek capital letters! The highly coloured passage ends:
its flames are fed by hell (verse 6). *Hell* here translates Greek
'ge-enna', Gehenna, the valley on the south-west of Jerusalem
where the rubbish fires burned and which became a symbol of
the place of eternal punishment. Another colourful sentence
follows. All kinds of living creatures—beasts, birds, reptiles,
fishes—*can be subdued and have been subdued by mankind; but no
man can subdue the tongue* (verses 7, 8). Most readers will feel

that the language now is becoming rhetorical rather than literal. So with verse 8*b*, *it is an intractable evil, charged with deadly venom*. This is sometimes the case, but fortunately not always so.

In verses 9–12, the writer gets on to a more sober estimate of the real problem of controlling the tongue, namely the difficulty of attaining to real consistency in speech. The same tongue, he says, is used *to sing the praises of our Lord and Father* and *to invoke curses upon our fellow-men* (verse 9). The phrase *our Lord and Father* is to be found only here in the New Testament though 'God and Father' is very common. The phrase has a Christian ring about it, but it is anticipated here and there in the Old Testament, e.g. in Isa. 63: 16 'thou, O Lord, art our father'. The idea of incompatibility [*fresh and brackish water* (verse 11), *olives* being derived from the *fig-tree*, *figs* from *a vine* (verse 12)] is reminiscent of the words of Jesus in Matt. 7: 16, 'Can grapes be picked from briars, or figs from thistles?' There, however, the point is that incompatible fruit is *impossible*— good trees bring forth good fruit, evil trees evil fruit. Here, in James, the point is that it is wrong and sinful to allow bad deeds (or words or thoughts) to spring from the same source as that from which prayers and praises flow.

Behind all this stress on the tongue, there is one important truth. Words are the principal, almost the only medium whereby personalities come into meaningful touch with each other. Hence, they contribute vitally to the development and formation of the character of the speaker, as well as vitally influencing the lives of the hearers. Hence, in stressing the importance of the tongue, the writer is dealing with a very important aspect of human relationships. It is not, however, the only important aspect. The hand, the eye, the sexual nature, all have their own 'spheres of influence'. We must consider the whole of our nature, our personality as such, and not just isolated parts of our bodies, even important parts like the tongue. ✳

WISDOM TRUE AND FALSE

13 Who among you is wise or clever? Let his right conduct give practical proof of it, with the modesty that comes of

14 wisdom. But if you are harbouring bitter jealousy and selfish ambition in your hearts, consider whether your

15 claims are not false, and a defiance of the truth. This is not the wisdom that comes from above; it is earth-bound,

16 sensual, demonic. For with jealousy and ambition come

17 disorder and evil of every kind. But the wisdom from above is in the first place pure; and then peace-loving, considerate, and open to reason; it is straightforward and sincere, rich in mercy and in the kindly deeds that are its

18 fruit. True justice is the harvest reaped by peacemakers from seeds sown in a spirit of peace.

* A feature of James is its self-contained sections, only very loosely, if at all, attached to what has preceded or what follows. They are often isolated 'sermonettes'. They would have done for little talks on the radio had that existed in the first century! This passage is such a section. It is a little discussion about true wisdom. It begins with the rhetorical question *Who among you is wise or clever?* (verse 13). It would seem that claims to superior wisdom or knowledge were something of a nuisance, and needed checking. Perhaps those who claimed special knowledge were early exponents of that set of beliefs later known as *gnosticism*, with its claim to special insight into the ways of God with men (see p. 9 ff.). However that may be, James here distinguishes between the wisdom which belongs very much to this human, faulty world, and that which has a heavenly, or divine ring about it. The fatal symptoms are *bitter jealousy and selfish ambition* (verse 14). The wisdom or cleverness marked by such features is *earth-bound, sensual, demonic* (verse 15). These adjectives are in increasing order of undesirability. *Earth-bound* translates Greek *epigeios* which can mean just 'belonging to the earth'. Here, however, it contrasts with the idea of coming 'from above', from heaven. *Sensual* translates Greek *psychikē*, belonging to the psyche or animal soul, rather than to the higher nature, the *pneuma* or spirit—*sensual* hits off the slightly 'carnal' atmosphere of the Greek word. *Demonic* translates Greek *daimoniōdēs*. It means 'under the control of' or 'taking its form from' demons, evil spirits. It is interesting to see demonic influence connected with things like strife and jealousy rather than with physical defects (deafness, dumbness, paralysis, etc.) as we find in the Gospels. *Jealousy and ambition* (verse 16) are rightly said to produce *disorder and evil of every kind*.

Then comes the inevitable contrast: *the wisdom from above* (verse 17). Its characteristics are listed as purity, the love of peace, a considerate and reasonable spirit, honesty, sincerity, mercy and kindliness (verse 17). The list of 'virtues' is not very different from Paul's 'harvest of the Spirit' in Gal. 5: 22 ff.: 'love, joy, peace, patience, kindness, goodness, fidelity, gentleness, and self-control'. Curiously enough, this Pauline list of heavenly virtues follows immediately, in Galatians, on a list of earthly and sensual characteristics. It looks as though it was usual for Christian teachers to use this method of contrasting lists of virtues and vices when expounding 'the two ways'—of life and death. Verse 18 says that *True justice is the harvest reaped by peacemakers from seeds sown in a spirit of peace*. A more literal translation might read, 'the fruit which is justice comes from seed which is peacefully sown for the benefit of peace-lovers'. We are very near to the words of Jesus in Matt. 5: 9, 'How blest are the peacemakers; God shall call them his sons'. ✶

DANGERS OF AN ACQUISITIVE SOCIETY

What causes conflicts and quarrels among you? Do they **4** not spring from the aggressiveness of your bodily desires? You want something which you cannot have, and so you ₂

are bent on murder; you are envious, and cannot attain
your ambition, and so you quarrel and fight. You do not
3 get what you want, because you do not pray for it. Or,
if you do, your requests are not granted because you pray
from wrong motives, to spend what you get on your
4 pleasures. You false, unfaithful creatures! Have you never
learned that love of the world is enmity to God? Whoever
chooses to be the world's friend makes himself God's
5 enemy. Or do you suppose that Scripture has no meaning when it says that the spirit which God implanted in
6 man turns towards envious desires? And yet the grace he
gives is stronger. Thus Scripture says, 'God opposes the
7 arrogant and gives grace to the humble.' Be submissive
then to God. Stand up to the devil and he will turn and
8 run. Come close to God, and he will come close to you.
Sinners, make your hands clean; you who are double-
9 minded, see that your motives are pure. Be sorrowful,
mourn and weep. Turn your laughter into mourning and
10 your gaiety into gloom. Humble yourselves before God
and he will lift you high.

✲ The writer continues to provide isolated 'paragraphs'
usually introduced by a question or a clear indication of the
subject. Here he begins, *What causes conflicts and quarrels
among you?* (verse 1). The word translated *conflicts* usually
means 'wars', but possibly a more general sense—'conflicts'
—will do here. That is if the passage is to be taken as addressed
to individuals, and especially to Christians. It is a feature
of James that much of its material could be addressed to a
non-Christian audience, almost in the form of a general
moral challenge to society. In this respect the material is
like much of the teaching of Jesus as recorded in the Gospels.
It deals not with the Christian revelation as such, but is

itself part of the revelation, that part which consists of moral challenge.

Here we are told that *conflicts and quarrels* arise from insatiable *bodily desires* (verse 1). There is violent covetousness, leading to the subject being *bent on murder* (verse 2). The Greek does not say *bent on murder*, it says 'you murder'. It is admittedly strange to find a word of such violence in the middle of words like *envious* and *ambition*. If the passage is addressed not to individual Christians, but to 'the world', to society, it is more understandable. Murders and similar catastrophes *do* spring from unbridled lusts and uncontrolled jealousies, as is frequently shown in daily life.

At the end of verse 2, *You do not get what you want because you do not pray for it* makes an abrupt change in the tone. Praying is a long way from killing! It may be that here the writer turns to the more common problems of a Christian group. Either they do not pray for what they want, or they pray *from wrong motives* (verse 3) intending *to spend what* they *get on* their *pleasures*. The neglect of prayer, or the misuse of it, has always been a subject on which preachers and teachers have dwelt. The deduction must not be drawn that if they had asked, and asked from the best motives, they would have necessarily 'obtained their petitions'. Life is full of cases where these conditions have been fulfilled, but where the asked-for boon has not been forthcoming. Positively, however, there are abundant cases where 'effective prayer' (see 5: 16) has proved powerful. Matt. 7: 7 ('Ask and you will receive', etc.) makes great, but not exact promises as to what will be received in answer to prayer. Often, in the scriptural promises, the phrase 'in my name' occurs (see, e.g. John 16: 23, 'if you ask the Father for anything in my name, he will give it you'). This phrase means that the prayer must spring out of a close identification with Jesus—as though he were praying through his disciples' lips. This condition would rule out most self-centred prayers.

They are now addressed as *false, unfaithful creatures* (verse 4), a long equivalent for the Greek word for 'adulteresses'. It avoids the difficulty that the word used in the original is feminine, and there is no reason to confine these strictures to women. To avoid the difficulty, some MSS insert 'adulterers' before 'adulteresses', but all that is implied is a general charge of disloyalty and faithlessness.

The writer goes on: *love of the world is enmity to God* (verse 4). The world's friends, he says, are God's enemies. At this point James is very near to 1 John 2: 15, 'Anyone who loves the world is a stranger to the Father's love'. Notice the same argument, used in the reverse direction in John 19: 12 (in the trial of Jesus), 'If you let this man go, you are no friend to Caesar'.

Verse 5 is particularly difficult to translate and explain confidently. Notice the N.E.B. version: *Or do you suppose that Scripture has no meaning when it says that the spirit which God implanted in man turns towards envious desires?* The first difficulty here is that no one has been able to find any place in Scripture where this is said. There are many stories and sayings in which man's envy and selfishness are portrayed, as, e.g. the story of Cain and Abel (Gen. 4: 1–15). Perhaps it is material of this sort that James has in mind, though usually 'the scripture' means one particular text or sentence. Gen. 6: 5 is possibly in mind. The next difficulty is that many commentators have thought that *the spirit* means the Holy Spirit, who, Christians believed, had come to 'indwell' their hearts. It is better, however, with the N.E.B. to take *the spirit* in the sense of the living breath of life breathed into man to make him a 'living soul' (see Gen. 2: 7). This spirit, as the story of the Fall soon showed, turned *towards envious desires* (verse 5).

Verses 6–9 form a rhetorical climax to this section. Verse 6 quotes first two words (in the Greek) from Prov. 3: 34, in the Septuagint or Greek version of the Old Testament—he 'gives grace'. This grace is said to be *stronger* (than the natural temptation to envy and hatred). Then the whole verse from Proverbs is quoted: *God opposes the arrogant and gives grace to the*

humble. The very same text is quoted in 1 Pet. 5: 5. The
thought of God's assistance to the humble and meek is particularly prominent in the New Testament (see, e.g. the song
known as *Magnificat*, Luke 1: 46–55). A number of short,
arresting sentences follow. Submission to God is commanded
(verse 7) (cf. 1 Pet. 5: 6, 'Humble yourselves then under God's
mighty hand'). The devil must be resisted (verse 7); again
cf. 1 Pet. 5: 8. Sinners are called to cleansing (verse 8), the
'double-thinkers' to honest sincerity. Mourning, and re-
pentance for sin, are urged after the manner of the Old
Testament prophets (e.g. Joel 1: 17). *

DANGERS OF A FAULT-FINDING SOCIETY

Brothers, you must never disparage one another. He who 11
disparages a brother or passes judgement on his brother
disparages the law and judges the law. But if you judge
the law, you are not keeping it but sitting in judgement
upon it. There is only one lawgiver and judge, the One 12
who is able to save life and destroy it. So who are you to
judge your neighbour?

* This short section makes a curious point. It begins by telling
its readers not to *disparage one another* (verse 11). It proceeds to
say that the one who *disparages a brother or passes judgement on
his brother disparages the law* (verse 11). How can this be? The
only simple explanation is that *the law* which is spoken of is
'the law of Christ', the teaching of Jesus. We saw that James
thought of Christ's teaching as *the perfect law, the law that
makes us free* (1: 25) and as *the sovereign law* (2: 8). Christ's law
had plainly stated, 'Pass no judgement, and you will not be
judged' (Matt. 7: 1). To disobey this law by criticizing and
judging, was by implication a criticism of that law.

The reference to *the One who is able to save life and destroy it*
immediately recalls Matt. 10: 28, 'Fear him...who is able to

destroy both soul and body in hell'. It is another close link
between the *original* gospel material and this letter. ✻

'GOD WILLING WE SHALL LIVE TO DO THIS OR THAT'

13 A word with you, you who say, 'Today or tomorrow we
will go off to such and such a town and spend a year there
14 trading and making money.' Yet you have no idea what
tomorrow will bring. Your life, what is it? You are no
more than a mist, seen for a little while and then dispers-
15 ing. What you ought to say is: 'If it be the Lord's will,
16 we shall live to do this or that.' But instead, you boast and
17 brag, and all such boasting is wrong. Well then, the man
who knows the good he ought to do and does not do it is
a sinner.

✻ Here is an isolated section warning against over-confident
planning for the future. The illustration is taken from the
world of commerce. James has a dislike of 'the rich', and
turns naturally to the prosperous trading classes for an example
of what he dislikes. Some businessmen, he imagines, plan a
whole year's business expedition, which they expect to be
very profitable. James reminds them that life is short and
precarious. In a poetic vein, their life is described as *a mist,
seen for a little while and then dispersing* (verse 14). Instead of
boastfully bragging they *should* have said *If it be the Lord's will,
we shall live to do this or that* (verse 15). The literal following of
this instruction led old-fashioned Christians to insert the
letters D.V. (*Deo volente*, God willing) before any statement of
future plans. This could easily become a superstitious habit,
but the idea or habit of mind behind it is sound. Christian
life must always be shaped as God's plan and providence make
his will and purpose clear. The point made by James is much
like that made in the parable of Jesus about 'the rich fool'

(Luke 12: 16–21). 'The rich fool' planned a great extension to his farm buildings, to be followed by a life of selfish ease. He was brought up sharp by being told that that very night he must die. He learned too late that his life was *a mist, seen for a little while.* ✶

AN ATTACK ON THE RICH

Next a word to you who have great possessions. Weep 5 and wail over the miserable fate descending on you. Your 2 riches have rotted; your fine clothes are moth-eaten; your silver and gold have rusted away, and their very 3 rust will be evidence against you and consume your flesh like fire. You have piled up wealth in an age that is near its close. The wages you never paid to the men who 4 mowed your fields are loud against you, and the outcry of the reapers has reached the ears of the Lord of Hosts. You have lived on earth in wanton luxury, fattening your- 5 selves like cattle—and the day for slaughter has come. You have condemned the innocent and murdered him; 6 he offers no resistance.

✶ This interesting passage may throw light on much else in James. It will be noticed that individual sections of the letter have been addressed to different groups. Thus 3: 13–18 was addressed to the *wise or clever* (verse 13); 4: 1–10 to the quarrelsome and envious—the second person being used throughout most of the section, as though among the readers were murderers and fighters; 4: 13–17 was addressed directly to the over-confident businessmen. Now comes this section (5: 1–6) addressed directly to those *who have great possessions* (verse 1).

The more closely this passage is examined the less likely it seems to be that the writer of James expected people of the type he condemns to be among actual Christian readers of his tract. It is surely more probable that he had the rhetorical habit of giving his moral teaching or rebuke in the second person (*Weep and wail. . . your riches have rotted*, etc., verses 1, 2) much as the prophets of Israel had done (e.g. Isa. 28: 14, 'hear the word of the Lord, ye scornful men, that rule this people which is in Jerusalem'). Once this is seen and accepted, it is possible to see how a passage like this fits into the letter, and also how the writer could speak about murders and fights in 4: 1-10 without necessarily implying that these things went on in the actual Christian community he was addressing.

Now this section (5: 1-6) is a violent attack on the rich. In the early part the mere having of great possessions is sufficient, it seems, to bring the owners into condemnation. In verse 4, however, it is said that the mowers and reapers who worked for the rich men have not been paid their proper wages, and that the rich have lived lives of wanton luxury. While it could be said that apart from these obvious moral lapses the rich might not have come in for such attacks, it is more important to attempt to 'place' a passage like this against the social and religious background of New Testament times.

The first obvious point of interest is the close similarity of language between 2 and 3 and the words of Jesus in Matt. 6: 19. There Jesus says, 'Do not store up for yourselves treasure on earth, where it grows rusty and moth-eaten, and thieves break in to steal it'. Here, in James, we have the rich being told, *Your riches have rotted; your fine clothes are moth-eaten; your silver and gold have rusted away* (verses 2, 3). The words in the Greek are not as close as the N.E.B. makes them appear (e.g. *moth-eaten*, used in Matthew and James in the N.E.B. represents different Greek phrases in the two books). Nevertheless the suggestion that 'moth and rust' destroy and corrode material possessions is clear in both books.

The next point to make is that, quite apart from detailed literary parallels, there is much similarity between what is said in Jas. 5: 1-6 and what is often said or written of in the Gospels. Thus, for instance, the question of paying wages to reapers is raised in the parable of the labourers in the vineyard

(Matt. 20: 1–16). The idea of a rich farmer being overtaken by death and judgement occurs in Luke 12: 13–21. The Beatitudes, in what was probably their earlier form, contained the plain statement, 'How blest are you who are poor' (Luke 6: 20) and the corresponding condemnation, 'Alas for you who are rich' (Luke 6: 24). Undoubtedly in the earliest phase of the Christian movement there was a close identification with 'the poor' and a corresponding detachment from 'the rich'.

What did this really mean? One element in it was the tradition coming down from the late Judaistic period that 'the poor in the land' were special objects of God's care and more disposed to obey his law. Here 'the poor' were contrasted with the rich Sadducean families, who were tempted to compromise their Jewish loyalty in order to keep on good terms with the Roman overlords. But in the time of Jesus there was a school of thought which held that meticulous obedience to the law was necessary, and this (especially the observance of ritual) could be achieved more easily by the leisured rich than by the busy poor. So when Jesus said 'How hard it will be for the wealthy to enter the kingdom of God!' (Mark 10: 23), we read that, 'They were amazed that he should say this' (Mark 10: 24). The different streams of tradition get somewhat confused.

In the primitive church there were those who could sell 'houses and lands' for the cause, like Barnabas, and Ananias and Sapphira (Acts 4: 36 — 5: 2). Barnabas gave all his wealth, Ananias and Sapphira pretended to give all the proceeds of a sale, but gave only part. In 1 Tim. 6: 17 ff. the rich are shown how they can make use of their riches to help the poor, and how necessary it is for them not to get 'attached' to their material wealth. Mostly, however, the church members seem to have been poor. James says that God had chosen the 'poor in the eyes of the world to be rich in faith' (2: 5). Paul says of himself and his fellow-Christians (2 Cor. 6: 10): 'poor ourselves, we bring wealth to many; penniless, we own the world'. This was the essential attitude of the early Church —they had riches, but these riches were spiritual, not material.

In the passage now under discussion (Jas. 5: 1–6) there is special stress on the nearness of the end of the world. *You have piled up wealth in an age that is near its close* (verse 3). The literal translation is 'you have collected treasure in the last days'. Probably the N.E.B. has got at the real meaning, but this meaning soon became obscure in the early Church. By the time the Vulgate (Jerome's Latin translation of the Bible) was written (fourth century) they had put in the word 'wrath' (Latin *iram*) so that the meaning was 'you have piled up wrath in (or for) the last days'. Similarly, after the vivid picture of the rich *fattening* (themselves) *like cattle* (verse 5) it is stated that *the day for slaughter has come*. The N.E.B. has certainly 'improved' James at this point—the original is not so vivid or clear.

The question arises, where might there be rich classes to whom such words could be addressed? The district is agricultural, because there are the references to the mowers and reapers. In the ancient world, however, the biggest towns were not far from the country, so that does not help us much. The passage could have arisen in the same area as that in which the teaching of Jesus was given. There is nothing completely incompatible between the 'local colour' of the passage and that of the Gospels.

In the second century there was a Christian sect known as the Ebionites (poor men). They flourished east of the Jordan. They lived very ascetic lives, and held a 'reduced' doctrine about Jesus, i.e. they stressed the human side of his nature almost to the exclusion of the divine. They adhered to the Jewish law. One cannot help thinking that a passage like Jas. 5: 1–6 would fit in very well with Ebionite doctrine, and once that is granted, other passages (e.g. those which speak of 'the perfect law') could be thought of as indicative of the Ebionite attitude. Naturally this does not mean that James was a product of the school known as Ebionite; only that it may have emerged in circles which later gave rise to Ebionism.

We must still look at verse 6. *You have condemned the inno-*

cent and murdered him; he offers no resistance. Who was meant by *him*? Could it be Jesus? If so, the reference comes in very abruptly. Jesus is called 'the just one' in Acts 3: 14: 'you... repudiated the one who was holy and righteous' (Greek *dikaion* = just). The present tense *he offers no resistance*, or (literally) 'he offers no resistance to you', is curious if the reference is to Jesus. The N.E.B. has come down on the side of a more general meaning—that of innocent and helpless victims of social and financial oppression. ✶

PATIENCE UNTIL THE COMING OF THE LORD

Be patient, my brothers, until the Lord comes. The farmer 7 looking for the precious crop his land may yield can only wait in patience, until the winter and spring rains have fallen. You too must be patient and stout-hearted, for the 8 coming of the Lord is near. My brothers, do not blame 9 your troubles on one another, or you will fall under judgement; and there stands the Judge, at the door. If 10 you want a pattern of patience under ill-treatment, take the prophets who spoke in the name of the Lord; re- 11 member: 'We count those happy who stood firm.' You have all heard how Job stood firm, and you have seen how the Lord treated him in the end. For the Lord is full of pity and compassion.

✶ There is a possible connexion between this paragraph and the preceding one, in that this paragraph contemplates *ill-treatment* of Christians (verse 10) and that one considered the ill-treatment of the poor (verse 4). As usual, however, the link is very tenuous: we really have quite a new subject, the need of patience until the coming of Christ.

The different strata of the New Testament mostly give evidence of the expectation of the return of Jesus in power and glory. The Synoptic Gospels speak much of 'the coming of the Son of Man', and it is clear that as these stand they mean by this the coming of Jesus (see Matt. 24: 3, 'what will be the signal for *your* coming and the end of the age?'). The letters of Paul similarly look forward to 'the coming of the Lord Jesus Christ'. The phrase 'coming of the Lord' (without 'Jesus') is unusual. In addition to the two references in this short section of James (verses 7 and 8) it occurs only in 1 Thess. 4: 15. Both in Jas. 5: 7 and 1 Thess. 4: 15 the N.E.B. paraphrases *until the Lord comes* but in all three cases the Greek has 'the coming of the Lord', his presence, or arrival.

The section Jas. 5: 7–11 is one which could hardly have been written outside Christian circles, which cannot be said of much of James. It is true that the Old Testament contemplated a coming of the Lord (e.g. Ps. 98: 8, 9, 'Let the hills sing for joy together; Before the Lord, for he cometh to judge the earth'), but this familiar reference to 'the coming of the Lord' seems to indicate a specifically Christian hope. As there is so strong a stress on patience, there is a suggestion that the years are going by—if this is sound it suggests a later rather than an early date (cf. 2 Pet. 3: 4, 'they will say: "Where now is the promise of his coming?"'). The necessary patience is illustrated by the agricultural picture of waiting for *the winter and spring rains*. In Palestine the rain is concentrated in the period October to April, and within this period the winter (or early) rain comes in October and November: the spring (or latter) rain in March and April. If those rains failed, the farmer's situation was very serious. Hence his anxious *wait in patience* (verse 7).

James says that *the coming of the Lord is near*. 1 Pet. 4: 7 says, 'The end of all things is upon us'; Phil. 4: 6 says 'The Lord is near'. James repeats his statement in slightly different words: *there stands the Judge, at the door* (verse 9). According to human standards it would seem that all these writers were in the wrong. Two thousand years, or nearly so, have gone by without any apocalyptic event such as they contemplated. But the writer of 2 Peter already saw the kind of answer that would have to be made. 'Our fathers have been laid to their rest, but still everything continues exactly as it has always been since the world began'—so said the 'scoffers' in 2 Pet. 3: 4. To which the writer replied (2 Pet. 3: 8), 'here is one point, my friends, which you must not lose sight of: with the Lord one day is like a thousand years and a thousand years like one day'. God's time-scale is not the same as man's. Christians have to live as though the assertion of the rule of God in Christ was an immediate possibility. This 'concentrates the mind wonderfully', as Dr Johnson said of a very different situation.

By way of an example of patience, the writer points first to *the prophets who spoke in the name of the Lord* (verse 10). '*We count those happy who stood firm*' (verse 11). This last sentence is given as a quotation. The nearest Old Testament equivalent is Dan. 12: 12: 'Blessed is he that waiteth', but the writer may have known some quotation more exactly like his own words. Then, as a precise example he refers to 'the patience (or endurance) of Job'. The N.E.B. paraphrases the Greek and says 'how Job stood firm'—the familiar English phrase translated more literally what was in the original. Job was not a prophet in any exact sense of the term, but all Old Testament books and characters could be comprised under the general term 'prophets' (see Luke 24: 25). *How the Lord treated him in the end* (verse 11) is a bold paraphrase of a Greek phrase, 'the Lord's goal or climax,' meaning, as the N.E.B. rightly implies, the 'happy ending' which follows on Job's 'chapter of accidents' (see Job. 42: 7–end). Modern students usually consider the 'happy ending' of Job (derived probably from an underlying folk tale) something of an anticlimax; without it the story would have a tragic grandeur; but such thoughts were naturally far removed from writers of the first century A.D. *The Lord is full of pity and compassion* (end of verse 11) is almost an exact quotation from Psalm 103: 8. ✳

NO SWEARING

12 Above all things, my brothers, do not use oaths, whether
'by heaven' or 'by earth' or by anything else. When you
say yes or no, let it be plain 'Yes' or 'No', for fear that
you expose yourselves to judgement.

✳ Verse 12 is a section of James which comes very close to
being an actual quotation from Matthew. It is, however, very
slightly different. Matthew says (5: 34–7), 'You are not to swear
at all—not by heaven, for it is God's throne, nor by earth, for
it is his footstool, nor by Jerusalem, for it is the city of the
great King, nor by your own head, because you cannot turn
one hair of it white or black. Plain "Yes" or "No" is all
you need to say; anything beyond that comes from the devil'.
James says, *Above all things, my brothers, do not use oaths, whether
'by heaven' or 'by earth' or by anything else. When you say yes or
no, let it be plain 'Yes' or 'No', for fear that you expose yourselves
to judgement*. The references to 'heaven' and 'earth' (in the same
order) and the reference to 'Yes' and 'No' (even more similar
in the Greek than in the N.E.B.) make *some* literary connexion
between the two passages certain. This could arise from a
knowledge of Matthew by the author of James, or vice versa
(very unlikely) or because of a common oral tradition, known
to both, a tradition that even in Greek was beginning to take
on a fixed form.

With regard to the substance of the passage it will be re-
membered that the Jewish people had always paid special
attention to careless swearing, particularly when the Divine
Name was used. The third commandment was 'Thou shalt
not take the name of the Lord thy God in vain; for the Lord
will not hold him guiltless that taketh his name in vain'
(Exod. 20: 7). Such was the fear of irreverence that the
principal name for God (*Yahweh*) was never spoken in divine
service, but a substitute word (*Adonai* = Lord) was used

wherever Yahweh appeared in the Scriptures. Jesus, and James after him, laid the stress on the sincerity and integrity which should mark all speech. Such should the trust be between speakers that their 'Yes' or their 'No' should suffice. This is a matter where Christians have departed widely from any literal obedience to the words of the Gospel or the letter of James. The last of the Thirty-nine Articles of the Church of England is entitled 'Of a Christian man's oath'. It says, 'As we confess that vain and rash Swearing is forbidden Christian men by our Lord Jesus Christ, and James his Apostle, so we judge, that Christian Religion doth not prohibit, but that a man may swear when the Magistrate requireth, in a cause of faith and charity, so it be done according to the Prophet's teaching, in justice, judgement, and truth.' It may well be that the importance attached to 'swearing' in ancient times depended on a certain semi-magical belief about the effectiveness of taking 'the Name' on the lips, and that the situation is quite different today. It is, however, difficult to avoid the feeling that the use of oaths in court, to add reliability to what is said, is just what should be unnecessary if the words of Matthew and James were obeyed. The Quakers have rigidly adhered to James's teaching and do not use oaths in court. The words *Above all things* at the beginning of verse 12 seem to give an undue importance to the section. Possibly it originally was part of a discourse in which matters of even less importance were discussed. ✲

SICKNESS AND SIN

Is anyone among you in trouble? He should turn to 13 prayer. Is anyone in good heart? He should sing praises. Is one of you ill? He should send for the elders of the 14 congregation to pray over him and anoint him with oil in the name of the Lord. The prayer offered in faith will 15 save the sick man, the Lord will raise him from his bed, and any sins he may have committed will be forgiven.

16 Therefore confess your sins to one another, and pray for one another, and then you will be healed. A good man's
17 prayer is powerful and effective. Elijah was a man with human frailties like our own; and when he prayed earnestly that there should be no rain, not a drop fell on
18 the land for three years and a half; then he prayed again, and down came the rain and the land bore crops once more.

✴ This last paragraph but one in the letter is one which has had more influence on the life and customs of the Church than any other paragraph in James.

It begins with some terse questions and instructions. *Is anyone among you in trouble? He should turn to prayer* (verse 13). These words might occur in a modern sermon. *Is anyone in good heart? He should sing praises.* The word translated 'sing praises' really means 'let him strike the harp', but it is used elsewhere in the New Testament of singing praises, especially psalms. Then comes the most interesting verse (14). *Is one of you ill? He should send for the elders of the congregation to pray over him and anoint him with oil in the name of the Lord.* During the ministry of Jesus healings of all kinds are said to have taken place. His apostles were sent out with a commission to do the same kind of thing (see Matt. 10: 8). According to Mark 16: 17, 18 (not part of the true text of Mark, but that is irrelevant here) the believers, after the Ascension, were to be able to perform healings; 'the sick on whom they lay their hands will recover'. Miracles of healing are recorded in Acts, and their occurrence is implied in some of Paul's letters (e.g. 1 Cor. 12: 9, 10).

In James the 'miraculous' aspect is still there, but it is in process of being changed to a regular feature of the life of the Church. The sick man is to send for *the elders of the congregation* (verse 14). In the sixteenth century there were great arguments as to whether the Greek word *ekklēsia* should be translated 'church' or 'congregation'. The N.E.B. rings the changes, using 'congregation' here, 'church' in Matt. 16: 18. *Elders* are the leaders, the governing council, probably older in years as a first qualification, but rapidly becoming marked out for certain qualities and gifts, which could, but did not always include teaching and preaching (see 1 Tim. 5: 17). These elders will *pray over him* (verse 14) and *anoint him with oil in the name of the Lord.* The use of oil in sickness and after injury was common. The good Samaritan bathed the wounds of the injured traveller 'with oil and wine' (Luke 10: 34). This was ordinary medicinal first-aid. But in Mark 6: 13 we read that the apostles 'drove out many devils, and many sick people they anointed with oil and cured'. This is a symbolic or sacramental anointing, and this is what is involved in James. The symbolic use of oil by the Church has continued in varying forms to the present day. A growing number of clergy now make use of the laying-on of hands and anointing with oil as part of their ministry to the sick. Anointing before death ('extreme unction') has always been part of some Christian traditions.

The next part of the paragraph conveys the positive assurances that such treatment will be effective. *The prayer offered in faith will save the sick man* (verse 15). With the promise of physical restoration (*the Lord will raise him from his bed*) goes the promise of forgiveness—*any sins he may have committed will be forgiven.* It was common to associate sickness with sin. Jesus greeted the paralytic who was let down through the roof for healing with the words, 'My son, your sins are forgiven' (Mark 2: 5). But in the Fourth Gospel, Jesus rejects the view that all sickness springs from sin (see John 9: 3). The important point—then as now—is to realize that God desires the health and well-being of the whole man, body and soul. God's will is not always done, and death and disease have to be accepted as having some place in God's ordering of things. But the Church follows Jesus and his apostles in praying hopefully and faithfully for physical health and spiritual restoration.

Verse 16, *confess your sins to one another, and pray for one another, and then you will be healed*, is surely a rather loose and general summary of what has gone before. There is no reference here to 'going to confession' in the modern sense of that phrase, although the presence and prayers of the elders here prescribed naturally provided a kind of scriptural precedent for private confession, before a priest when that later became part of the Church's rule. *A good man's prayer is powerful and effective* (verse 16). The main point of this is plain enough, but behind the word 'effective' there lies a big argument. The Greek word could mean 'when energized' (i.e. by God or the Holy Spirit). Most scholars have taken it in that way, but evidently the N.E.B. translators preferred the general sense of 'effective'. The N.E.B. is in any case a little free in translation here; *is powerful* does not quite convey the force of the Greek, which literally is, 'strong enough for much is the prayer of a just man when energized', or when it is energizing, i.e. when it is *energetic* or effective.

The section ends, as often, with one biblical example of the lesson that has been taught. Here it is the case of Elijah that is brought forward as an example of a man whose prayer worked. The reference is to the story in I Kings 17 and 18. The example counted for much in the mind of the writer of James, but modern readers cannot help asking, 'Did it really happen?' and 'Was it anything to do with Elijah's prayer?' That 'prayer changes things' is the universal experience of devout Christians of all centuries, but that one man's prayer could suspend the normal course of the weather for three and a half years is a part of the biblical tradition about which modern readers may reverently hold their own opinions. ⁎

WANDERERS MUST BE SOUGHT AND RESTORED

19 My brothers, if one of your number should stray from the
20 truth and another succeed in bringing him back, be sure
of this: any man who brings a sinner back from his

crooked ways will be rescuing his soul from death and cancelling innumerable sins.

✻ This rather stern letter ends on a note of compassion for the lost. Those who *stray from the truth* (verse 19) should be brought back by the efforts of the faithful. Anyone who thus restores a sinner *will be rescuing his soul from death and cancelling innumerable sins* (verse 20). There are ambiguities in the very last words of the letter. Whose soul is saved, and whose sins are cancelled? Those of the restored wanderer, or those of the restorer? Much ink can be spilled in support of either case, but the most natural meaning is that the one who is restored is the one whose soul is saved and whose sins are 'covered' (i.e. obscured, hidden). After all he *certainly* needed saving; the 'saver' is presumably not in so dire a plight. Moreover, saving others as a means to being saved oneself, would not seem a very attractive form of service for others! *Cancelling innumerable sins* (literally, 'covering' them) is a phrase which goes back to Prov. 10: 12, 'love covereth all transgressions'. 1 Peter quotes the same passage (1 Pet. 4: 8), 'love cancels innumerable sins'. Some early Fathers of the Church suggest that Jesus used this phrase. If so, it is one of his unrecorded sayings, although the popular interpretation of Luke 7: 47 might support the tradition. In that passage the N.E.B. avoids the usual interpretation by saying 'her great love *proves* that her many sins have been forgiven'. The older translations were more ambiguous, e.g. (A.V.), 'Her sins, which are many, are forgiven; for she loved much'. ✻

✻   ✻   ✻   ✻   ✻   ✻   ✻   ✻   ✻   ✻   ✻   ✻   ✻

INDEX OF
NAMES AND TOPICS

The references are to pages

Antichrist, 7, 11, 30, 31, 43, 46, 65
Asia, 16
Athanasius, Festal Letter of, 3, 92
Augustine, 3

Beloved Disciple, 3
brothers (= neighbours), 8, 40, 52

Carthage, Council of, 3
Cerinthus, 10, 66
Clement of Alexandria, 5, 80
Clement of Rome, 6, 22
Codex Sinaiticus, 3

Dead Sea Scrolls, 9, 20
Demetrius, 12, 62, 71, 72
Diotrephes, 12, 62, 69, 70, 71
Dispersion, the (= *diaspora*), 97
docetism, 9–11, 46

Ebionites, 132
ekeinos, 23
Ephesus, 10, 16
Eusebius, bishop of Caesarea, 5, 10, 71, 80, 92

faith, 49
faith and works, 112–17
Fourth Gospel, 3, 13–15

Gaius, 11, 12
Galatians, 92, 93, 94, 123
gnosticism, 9–11, 122

Hegesippus, 81, 82
Helvidius, 83
hilasmos, 21, 48

Ignatius, 16
Irenaeus, 5, 9, 71

James, Letter of, parallels with other New Testament writings, 84–91
    authorship, 93–5
James, son of Alphaeus, 75, 77
James, son of Zebedee, 75–7
James, the Lord's brother (the Just), 75, 78–83
Jerome, 4, 83
Johannine letters, authorship of, 13–16
John, son of Zebedee, 4
John the presbyter ('the elder'), 4, 12, 14–15, 62–5, 67–8

light (and darkness), 7–8, 24–5
love, 34–42, 49–53

Mary of Clopas, 77
Mary of Magdala, 76, 77
Mary, the mother of James and Joseph, 76, 83
Mary, the mother of Jesus, 77, 83
Matthew, Gospel of, 84–7, 94
Mayor, J. B., 89
Mommsen Canon, 4
Muratorian Fragment, 5, 91

neighbours (= brothers), 8, 40, 52

Origen, 5, 92

Papias, 5, 11
parakletos, 21
parallax, 104
parousia, 34
parrhesia, 42
Paul, 90–1
Peter, First Letter of, 87–90
Philo, 20, 38
Plato, 9

INDEX OF NAMES AND TOPICS

Polycarp, 6, 10, 14

prophecy, true and false, 43–7

synagogue, 110

Syria, 4

Re

P

S

S

s

s

DATE DUE
